THE OCCIDENTAL
1879 TO 2009
A WYOMING FRONTIER HOTEL

BY GIL BOLLINGER

In Memoriam

This book is dedicated to the memory of John Wexo who, with his loving wife Dawn, owned the Occidental Hotel. He was an author and publisher *par excellence*. His *Zoo Book* series sold in the hundreds of thousands, received multiple awards, and was translated into several foreign languages for sale abroad. Perhaps even more importantly, they delighted generations of children, introducing them to the world's animal kingdom, thereby contributing to their education. Appropriately, John was an observant naturalist and astute historian. He was also deeply concerned with historic preservation.

John was involved with this book's initial manuscript only in its very earliest phase. He enjoyed critiquing and editing. We both looked forward to working together with its writing and publication. His death robbed all of us of the benefits his collaboration would have provided. I found it a pleasure to know and to work with him. Along with his family and friends, I will miss him.

A Cowboy Poem

Where the Virginian Got His Man

Come on Boys, an' ride with me
For a Trip back to the Past.
We'll stop at the Occidental,
And step through the Looking Glass.

Here everything's just as it was
In a far, different age
When the Occidental wrote the Rules
On Hist'rys unwrote Page.

Her very name means "Western"
This fine ol' Grand Hotel.
Where workin' hands, who ride for Brands
Rub elbows with the Swells.

She sits at the foot of the Big Horns
In a regal splendor there,
She's the aging Queen o' the Prairies
With Roses in her Hair.

Now priceless Orientals
Still grace the well-worn floor
And Crystal Chandeliers
Still hang above the doors.

There's china in the Dining Room,
And everything's First Class
Where the Present is overshadowed
By reflections of the Past.

The floor still creaks and History reeks
'Til you can hear the Coyotes call,
And the Ghosts of Cattle Barons
Still roam the Hallowed Halls.

Here deals were made as cattle herds
And ranches all changed hands,
And famous cowboys singers
Have played their one-night Stands.

She was lost one night, in a Poker game
By a man with a Second-best Hand
And her walls are lined with Pictures
Of Men who, they say, had Sand.

Now the little Gal who owns the place
Is a genuine Western Buff,
And to make your stay more Pleasant
She simply can't do Enough.

Many a trail-worn Drifter
Has stopped here feeling Rough,
And when a Cowboy's broke n' Hungry
She'll write it on the Cuff.

Mister Wister holed up here
And dreamed a Master Piece
In an upstairs room by a Fireplace
Where mem'ry still had Lease.

Butch and Sundance slept here, too
Tom Horn got drunk, they say,
An' bragged he'd kill every Cow-thief
That did not ride Away.

It's faraway and Mystical
In a Place called Cowboy Land -
It's the Occidental Hotel
Where the Virginian got his Man.

Dan Hess, 2005

The Occidental

1879 to 2009

A Wyoming Frontier Hotel

Contents

A government photographer who had come to Buffalo to take official photographs of Fort McKinney apparently couldn't pass up taking a picture of this fine structure.

Source: Occidental Hotel and Museum Collection

The Occidental Hotel – circa 1880

This excellent photograph attests to Buell's skills as a carpenter. The hotel is obviously well made with log construction for the first floor and milled lumber for the second floor. The gambrel roof with its dormer windows and the two side buildings were distinctive and would become its trademark appearance. There was a livery with stables in the rear; its entrance with an overhead sign is shown in the upper enlargement.

Introduction

Early in the development of many western frontier towns, an obvious need for lodging and food by newcomers and travelers made the establishment of a hotel an attractive business endeavor. A number of those early operations prospered, became the "face of their community," and continued on well past the frontier era. The Occidental Hotel in Buffalo, Wyoming, is an example of the long-lasting type.

From its 1879 beginning in tents, to an 1880 log structure, then a new brick structure in 1910, and, lastly, a late 1990s restoration and development as a museum, the Occidental has grown with its host community. More than just the face of Buffalo, the hotel has become an integral part of the town's character and personality to both residents and visitors. One hundred-thirty years at the same site is testimonial to the Occidental's ongoing service.

The following pages will trace the hotel's history through that multi-generational period. Much of the early history is based on the family lore of founder Charles Buell. The same is also true for the later and much longer Smith family's ownership era. Newspaper articles help to a certain extent but much reliance has to be placed on what family members have written and the records and photos they have retained. With respect to the hotel's records themselves, they are extensive but, understandably, many important documents have been lost over the years. Fortunately, more than enough has been archived to allow a complete story to be told.

The Buell Family – 1895
Charles, holding the youngest son, Miles W., and Jennie Buell with their
children (left to right): Clarence, Frances L., Helen E., and Mabel G.

Source: Eldon Buell collection

The Buell Years – 1879-1888

The beginning of The Occidental Hotel, near the base of Wyoming's Big Horn Mountains could not have been more humble – a couple of tents and perhaps a canvas fly over a table and benches. It was started by Charles Edwin Buell (1855-1916) along Clear Creek near the eastern boundary of the Fort McKinney military reservation in the summer of 1879. As would be expected, virtually all that is known concerning that origin is derived from Buell family lore and records. One brief, but independent, account comes from John R. Smith, Johnson County pioneer and rancher. His description is as follows:

> Charles Buell and A. J. McCray [a later partner] started a hotel which consisted of some tepee poles with a wagon cover stretched over the top. This served as kitchen and dining room. In addition, there was a big tent for beds; thus the Occidental Hotel began.[1]

The reason for Buell and his boarders-to-be being at the Clear Creek location was the presence of the newly-sited Fort McKinney some three miles west of the fledgling hotel. The fort was named to honor a young lieutenant killed by Cheyenne warriors at the Dull Knife Battle, November 1876, in southern Johnson County. The military post had relocated from its initial Powder River site just east of the present-day community of Kaycee to the Clear Creek site during the summer of 1878. That change was to take advantage of the better water and lumber resources found in the Big Horns. It was one of several forts established by General Crook in Montana and Wyoming at the beginning of the reservation era for the Northern Plains tribes. The posts were to exhibit a military presence in the Lakota and Cheyenne's northern high plains traditional hunting grounds and to monitor any off-reservation travel. Additionally, the forts would provide protection from Indians to any local settlers as well as a market for their goods and services. These advantages were a strong incentive for ranchers, homesteaders, and farmers to settle near the new Fort McKinney garrison of some 300 soldiers. Military installations have always fostered the development of adjacent "army towns" and Fort McKinney was no exception. The Homestead Acts were in place and many Americans were coming west to take advantage of them. A military fort gave such homesteaders a source for cash income that enormously increased the likelihood that they would "prove up" and secure title to their land. Buell's tents were a part of a new community that was already developing rapidly – an embryonic community, Buffalo, with an embryonic hotel – the Occidental.

Helen Buell, eldest daughter of Charles, gave the earliest account of how her father got into the hotel business:

> He [Buell] had hardly settled in his tent when a group of miners came along. They asked if they might board with him for a few days. Buell agreed to accommodate them, for he was an excellent cook. The miners had come down from the Big Horn Mountains, and had some gold they had mined in the mountains.
>
> One of the men asked Buell if there was someplace (bank) where they could put the gold. Buell led them to the back of the tent and pulled a buffalo robe off the ground, where a hole had been dug. The gold was put into the hole and the robe pulled back over it. The miners stayed several days and ate delicious meals prepared by Buell, of bacon, eggs, flapjacks, and coffee. When they left, Buell was liberally rewarded for his hospitality. This could be considered the first hotel in Buffalo, and in fact, the beginning of the famous Occidental.[2]

This story of miners finding gold in the Big Horns is entirely possible but not at all typical. Time would prove that there were no large deposits of the precious metal in that mountain range. Several small to modest strikes were made over the years, accompanied by much speculation, but nothing substantial or long lasting. Wyoming historian Robert A. Murray stated in his 1981 book *Johnson County: 175 Years of History at the Foot of the Big Horns* that, "It seems safe to say that no search for metallic minerals in the Big Horns has *ever* paid even wages to the people who financed it."

Buell then decided the hotel business would be profitable and started the construction of a large, log structure to serve that purpose. However, he first had to build himself a temporary frame shack.[3] While clearing the underbrush and trees from the site, he is reported to have discovered a human skull that was firmly encased

Buell Family Photographs
Upper: Charles and Jennie – 1914. Lower: Miles W. Buell and wife Helen in the front seat with Charles and Jennie in the rear seat. The Model T Ford shown in this 1915 photograph is the one in which both of the elder Buells were killed in an accident the following year. Inset: License plate from the 1915 Buell automobile.

Sources: Upper and Lower – Eldon Buell collection; Inset: Author's collection.

by a group of branches in one of the trees. It was assumed that it began as an Indian scaffold burial and that the skull happened to have been held in position over time while the corpse and scaffold remains decayed, fell away, and were dispersed by the elements.

The new Occidental building was 24 feet by 28 feet and constructed by Buell who was a carpenter. It was completed during the fall of 1880. The lower floor housed the lobby, dining room, and kitchen. Six bedrooms, each with a dormer window, were on the upper floor. Ground level additions were added to the north and south sides, each with two rooms that, along with the main building's distinctive gambrel roof, gave the structure an attractive symmetry. The necessary stable and livery (rear) and hitching rack (front) completed the new, ten-bedroom facility.

As the dominant public structure in Fort McKinney's new and rapidly growing "army town," the Occidental quickly became more than just a hotel: it served as the Rock Creek-Junction City stage-coach station, a post office (Buell was the second postmaster with a salary of $16 per year),[5] a community gathering place and social center, the town hall, the main polling place, a hospital, and the county courthouse. On March 29, 1881, the newly-appointed commissioners, John R. Smith, Ray Park, and Charles A. Farwell, met in the Occidental's north wing to organize the new county.

Folklore and the Buell family tradition have it that the name for the new community was drawn from a hat by the town residents present in the Occidental saloon in 1880. The name Buffalo, submitted by a native of Buffalo, New York, was drawn.[6] In the hat drawing event, William Hart from Buffalo, New York, claimed to have deposited the slip of paper that was drawn. Miles Buell, grandson of Charles, told the author that the selection was not made by a single drawing but rather by the majority votes, and Buffalo won with two or more slips in the hat. I. S. Bartlett in his *History of Wyoming* states a different version as derived from Alvin J. McCray, Buell's partner-to-be. McCray was born in Buffalo, New York, in 1854 and came west at age 21. In 1876 he established his first hotel in Deadwood, South Dakota, but soon afterward came to Johnson, then Pease County. He supposedly assisted in laying out the county seat and named it after his New York home. It is not clear exactly what "laying out" means here; the town was not platted until 1884.

It appears certain, however, that Buffalo was not named for the millions of shaggy animals that once occupied the Great Plains region for millennia.

Buell took Alvin J. McCray as his partner and co-owner of the Occidental in 1881, presumably because of McCray's previous hotel management experience and perhaps also for capital input. McCray married Vinnie M. Keeler on February 28, 1886, in Johnson County. The McCrays had a daughter born April 6, 1887, while he was serving as one of the three county commissioners of Johnson County.[7]

Buell had married Jennie B. Herrick (1859-1916); both were natives of Wisconsin, on October 17, 1882, four years earlier. The couple would have five children – three girls and two boys. The first, Helen "Hallie" Elizabeth, was born August 4, 1883, in Buffalo. She is usually said to be the first white child born in Buffalo but that claim has been challenged. The *Buffalo Bulletin*, September 28, 1933, printed a letter from Mrs. H. W. Menth of Los Angles, California, who claims that she was born Louisa G. on December 20, 1882, the daughter of Mr. and Mrs. John A. Fischer, in their log cabin by the Fischer Brewery on Clear Creek in Buffalo. She points out her birth date is seven months and four days older than her dear friend, Hallie E. Buell.

The Occidental had two "first cooks," according to the available records, and each of them met an untimely, violent demise. The earliest, according to John R. Smith:

> ... was a gentleman of color named Thomas Jefferson. The cookhouse consisted of a couple of cottonwood forks and a stringer pole. This also provided a bedroom for Thomas Jefferson and a shelter for the government beans, "flitch" or bacon and other grub.[8]

It seems that Jefferson got into a gunfight with a cowboy named Pat Ragan and wounded him. Ragan was taken to the hospital at Fort McKinney (another service provided to the new community) for treatment. He later rode to Smith's ranch on Crazy Woman Creek, some 22 miles distant, where he stayed in the bunkhouse. Two days later, Jefferson appeared at the Smith ranch, reason unknown, seeking breakfast. When they saw each other, Ragan and Jefferson again began shooting. When the gun smoke cleared from a total of eleven shots, Jefferson had five bullets in him and *"... that being more lead than he could conveniently carry, he passed in his checks."* Ragan was also hit once, "The bullet had hit a rib opposite the heart and glanced off, making a small wound." Jefferson was buried and Ragan healed.

The second "first cook" was an emigrant German settler, Jacob "Dutch" Schmerer who was bludgeoned to death in 1885 by

John Owens (a.k.a. Bill Booth), a hired worker on Schmerer's home-stead. Supposedly, Schmerer had intended to provide the Occidental's restaurant menu with some venison that Owens was to deliver. When Owens did not deliver the game, an argument ensued that led to the killing. Owens then fled the area, was later apprehended in Montana, and returned to Buffalo for trial. He was convicted and, on March 5, 1886, legally hanged on a specially constructed scaffold behind the county courthouse. It was Johnson County's only hanging.[9]

The year 1884 was an important one for the Occidental as it finally acquired legal title to the land it had been occupying. Juliet Hart, widow of Fort McKinney's recently deceased commandant, Major Verling K. Hart, was awarded his Desert Land Claim patent that included all of the Buffalo community. Major Hart had filed his claim against the east boundary of McKinney's military reservation – exactly where Buffalo was starting to develop. As was typical during the frontier era, the people in Buffalo had settled where they wished with no thought to land ownership. That was usually settled later by claiming squatter's rights and/or by joint community action. When Juliet hired surveyors to prepare a town plat of streets and lots, it became clear to Buffalo's residents that she was claiming ownership of the entire town. They petitioned the Department of Interior in Washington, D.C. to have her patent rescinded but were unsuccess-ful. Everyone's homesites and business locations now belonged to Hart and they all became illegal squatters! They then had to deal with her for the purchase of the real estate they were occupying.[10]

Buell and McCray purchased the land the hotel was occupying from her. The Occidental sale was dated October 14, 1884. A large, south-side annex to the hotel on the Clear Creek side was also built that year.[11] No direct reason for this addition was noted but ostensi-bly it was to enhance business.

By the mid-1880s, the Buell hospitality at the Occidental was be-coming well known. During the winter of 1883, they held a masquerade ball, reputedly the first of its kind in Buffalo. Music provided by Fort McKinney's excellent Fifth Cavalry band added to the affair. Over 20 couples, *en masque*, took part in the grand march at eight o'clock and at nine o'clock the largest attendance of the season was present. Among the attendees were a Scotch Highlander, Devil, Clown, Indians, Sailor, Jesuit Irishman, King of Hearts, School Girl, Indian Maiden, Country Maiden, Mother Hubbard, Red and White Dominoes, Skating Girl, etc. The great unmasking took place at one o'clock to much fanfare.

A letter to the editor of the *Laramie Daily Boomerang* stated that the affair "vindicated Buffalo's metropolitan position in northern Wyoming."

There were also dances where an orchestra of Italian musicians played; when the dances were held in another hall, supper was often served afterwards at the Occidental.[12]

About 1885, Buell and McCray acquired a small hotel in south Buffalo from a Mr. Brunhaus. They converted it into a family hotel, named the Murray Hill Hotel, and advertised it as having "special accommodations for families."[13] Presumably, it did not have a saloon where cowboys could get a little rowdy. Little is known about this establishment or its operation. A local saying in Buffalo gave the choice between their two hotels as "Murray Hill or Merry Hell."

As expected, the Occidental had a saloon from its earliest days. It was a true western, frontier saloon and probably deserved the description above. Another early Buffalo resident is said to have described it as a "gambling hell" in reference to the many games there. The saloon in a small Western town has been well established in the many films about cowboys; they ranged from dives to elegant taverns and were a central meeting place for residents and travelers. The Occidental saloon did not start as low as a dive but evolved with time. It did and still does to this day have the requisite "batwing doors." Referred to as saloon, tavern, and bar, this was an important part of the history of the Occidental Hotel.

There is no record of any shootings at the Occidental during these early years but a stabbing there was noted in the *Big Horn Sentinel* of December 10, 1887. The assistant foreman of the Pratt & Ferris Ranch, Ben Kidwell, was stabbed by a man named Lane. The incident apparently resulted from the continuation of an ongoing quarrel between the two men. The wounds were not considered serious but Lane was arrested; he put up a bond of $200 and was scheduled to see Police Justice Parmelee that same day. A report on his judgment was not found.

Starting from these early years, the Occidental served as an unofficial "trauma center" for Johnson County. That is, anyone who was badly injured or became ill in the Buffalo vicinity was brought directly to the hotel where first aid was administered while a local doctor, or Fort McKinney's military surgeon, was sent for. In some cases the injured party would even convalesce in a hotel room under the care of the hotel staff or a family member. The following example is typical of both the services provided by the Occidental and of the type of events that could occur in the Big Horn Mountain region during Wyoming winters.

The principal here is Ed Wilhams, a local cowboy who had worked at the 76 Ranch. He wrote a letter in the mid-1930s describing an 1887 experience to his friend, Robert Foote, Jr., son of Buffalo's pioneer merchant.

> ...On Oct 17, 1887, I left Ten Sleep, horseback, also with a packhorse, for a trip over Buffalo-way. It was a warm day and I was dressed in summer attire. Up near Ten Sleep Lake, that evening, it began to snow. It snowed all night. I made a tent of my tarp and stayed there a day, otherwise I should probably have got lost in the clouds and snow. One evening late it cleared and, being short of grub, I pulled out, hoping to go to Uncle Billy Robinson's cabin (no one lived there, but it had a fireplace and was shelter from the storm and weather). Near midnight it got very cold. While crossing a stream, my horse fell in. The water froze to my clothes without running off. Well, when I got to the cabin my legs were frozen solid. I managed to get on my horse somehow, next morning, and to ride to Coachy's Canyon Ranch (North Fork Powder). It took me all day. The next day I rode on to the 76 on South Fork of Crazy Woman. "Deaf" Bennett went with me. After dark when we arrived. Went from there to Buffalo in a buckboard. I think it was Fred Hesse that took me – not sure, as I was about worn out with pain and loss of sleep. Arrived at the Occidental after midnight. Big poker game in the bar room. Miles Standish and old Lum Williams carried me to a down-stairs bedroom and sent for Dr. Lott. Doc smeared a barrel of carbolic cosmoline [a petroleum based substance] over my legs and padded me in cheese cloth and bandages.
>
> A few days alter when the flesh began to rot and when you could smell the carbolic acid for a town block, Mrs. Buell concluded that I should be moved just across the narrow alley, into a log cabin room, which was next to hers. There, later, Dr. Lott and an army doctor did some carving on me. I was in bed for 13 weeks, and it was another month before I could leave my room...

In addition to his amazingly positive outlook on life, Wilhams was also a rather literate cowboy.

After a decade of hotel management, Buell was apparently ready for a change. On March 10, 1888, he sold his share of the Occidental to partner McCray and his wife, Vinnie. The Buell family then moved to a ranch located in the Shell Creek-Lake DeSmet area, northwest of Buffalo. The Buells had filed the first two homestead applications in Johnson County; they were finally awarded in 1891. [14]

Charles Edwin Buell Genealogy

Because of Charles Buell's importance to the history of the Occidental Hotel, the first two generations of his family line are included here. Sources: Librarian Nancy Jennings, Johnson County Library, Buffalo, Wyoming and Eldon Buell, Sheridan, Wyoming.

Charles Edwin Buell (1855-1916) was born on July 25th in Bloomfield, Wisconsin.

Parents: William Ira Buell (New York) and Frances M. Matthews (Ohio)

Siblings: Seven brothers who did not die as an infant or young child: George Allen (1858), Ira, Luther, Mathew, Frank, John, and William.

Wife: Jennie B, Herrick (1859-1916; Wisconsin) – marriage on October 17,1882 in Wisconsin.

Children: Three daughters and two sons; listed in birth sequence: Helen E. (Hallie), Mabel G., Frances L., Clarence A., Miles W.

Second Generation

Helen E. (Hallie) Buell – born August 4, 1883 in Buffalo, Wyoming. Married Pool – three children.

Mabel G. Buell – Born in Buffalo, Wyoming – Married Winingar – four children.

Frances L. Buell – Born in Buffalo, Wyoming – Married Heacock – three children.

Miles W. Buell – Born in Buffalo, Wyoming – Married Helen on September 1, 1915. Seven sons and two daughters: Charles E. (2nd) (1916-2010), Frances (1917-2008), Harold T. (1919-2001), Miles (Jr.) (1920-2006), Beverly Katherine (1921-1994), John William (May to July, 1926), Walter E. (1928-1992), Ralph L. (1930), and Eldon I. (1931).

The Occidental Roof and the Trabing Store Building

Charles Buell was a talented carpenter. Two examples of his ability are the Occidental roof and the Trabing Store building.

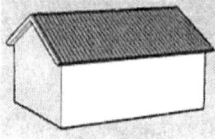
Gable Roof

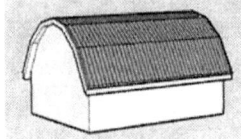
Gambrel Roof

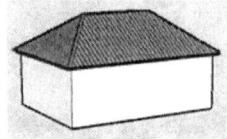
Hip Roof

   The 1880 Occidental's gambrel roof was quite unusual in frontier Wyoming. Virtually all of the structures at that time had gable roofs, the simplest type. Such was the case at Fort McKinney with its 30 to 40 buildings; the largest number to be found in northern Wyoming at the time. Buffalo's buildings, with time, would have the same gable roof and some of them also included the false fronts that were popular during the era.

   The gambrel roof, with its shallow slopes above steeper ones, was popular on eastern barns as it allowed for larger haylofts in the upper floor. Charles Buell probably learned the roofing technique in his native Wisconsin prior to immigrating to Wyoming. With the addition of dormer windows, both room space and light were added to his new hotel's second floor – and, he had a distinctive building profile.

The Occidental Roof and the Trabing Store
Source: Occidental Hotel and Museum Collection

   The above illustration, from the Buffalo Bulletin, August 9, 1951, is thought to be the oldest photograph of early Buffalo.

It is dated at 1879. The first two lines of its newspaper cap-tion read:

First Buffalo store moved piece by piece from Trabing, one of the first settlements in Johnson County. The late C. E. Buell and his associates moved the building into Buffalo when this was known as Pease County, before it became Johnson.

The Trabing brothers, Augustus (1842-1906) and Charles (1845-1885) were pioneer merchants who hold a special place in the earliest histories of Wyoming, Johnson County, and Buffalo. Their trading post was a roadhouse established on Crazy Women Creek, some 20 miles south of fledging Buffalo, in 1878. On the freighting route from Cheyenne to the Powder River forts, it developed into an early gathering site for travelers. In 1879, August Trabing, Charles Buell, and three other men decided to construct another store near Buffalo to take advantage of its developing markets and those at Fort McKinney. Due to uncertainty as to the exact location of the eastern boundary of the military reservation for Fort McKinney, they built a large structure, similar to the one at Crazy Woman Creek and shown above, south of Buffalo in the Six Mile or Cross H Ranch area. When the boundary question was settled they moved the new building to Buffalo and sited it some 15 feet above the Clear Creek bed, in the location of the present day First National Bank The new building was described as primitive but very sturdy with the boards put together with pegs instead of nails and the hand-made shingles. It was stocked as a true "general store" in the frontier sense – if an item was needed or wanted, it was almost certainly in the store. In early 1882, Trabing sold out to J. H. Conrad and Company and they took over operation of the store.

The Trabing-Buell connection extends back to Wisconsin. The Laramie newspapers reported that August Trabing made numerous buying trips back "East" in 1878. The year before, his wife Ulrika's younger half-sister, Hannah Raduchal had come from Wayside, Wisconsin, to care for the Charles Trabing children. Apparently, a relationship developed between August and Hannah. She returned to Wisconsin at the close of 1877 and August's trips were ostensibly to see her. August and Ulrika subsequently filed divorce papers that became final in September, 1880. August and Hannah were mar-ried shortly thereafter.

In 1878, Buell left his Wisconsin home to accompany August on his return to Johnson County, apparently as his employee. He remained so until he started his hotel on Clear Creek.[4]

Occidental Hotel Annexes – circa early 1880s

The above two photographs show the two annexes that were built on the south side (left) near Clear Creek. The upper photograph appears to be the earlier with the oxen-team freight wagons on Main Street. The lower photograph depicts a tall flagpole and a large number of men, posing in front of the larger annex. The Occidental Stables are seen against the right edge of this photograph.

Source: Occidental Hotel and Museum collection

Stagecoach Stop – circa early 1880s

One of the Occidental's many functions was a stagecoach stop. The earliest line to use the hotel was the Rock Creek-Junction City Line. Over time, the operation of individual lines would come and go; apparently they all used the Occidental's convenient food, lodging, and livery services on Buffalo's Main Street. The photograph above has two stagecoaches in front of the hotel with a large number of citizens posing for the photographer. The unusual occasion of a photographer and the length of time it took to set their camera up were more than adequate for the townsfolk to gather, including at a second-story window.

Source: Occidental Hotel and Museum collection

Political Committee Meeting Place – 1884

The Minutes (right) are for the September 23, 1884 meeting of the Central Committee of the Republican Party. Its purpose was to call a Republican Convention and select 44 delegates from the northern Wyoming area.

Source: Occidental Hotel and Museum collection

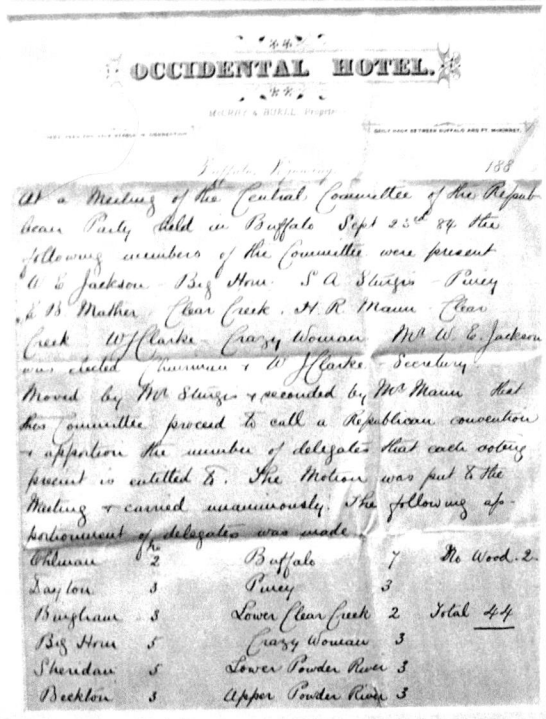

Bill Booth – Killer, Escape Artist, and Poet

Bill Booth, aka John Owens, was apparently an intelligent, talented man but with an uncontrollable temper and/or a complete lack of social morality. Arriving in Buffalo in 1884, he was described as being about 5´10˝ tall with black hair and a generally clean-cut appearance. His 1885 murder of his employer, Dutch Schmerer, was particularly brutal – he hit him several times on the head with a hatchet. Booth immediately fled the area but was apprehended in Montana and returned to Johnson County by Sheriff Frank M. Canton. There he was tried, convicted of murder in the first degree, and sentenced to death by hanging on July 11, 1885. The execution date was set as March 5, 1886. The reason for that long time separation is not known.

Bill Booth aka John Owens
Hanged for murder at Buffalo,
Johnson County, Wyoming
Territory, on March 5, 1886.
Source: Modified after a Pencil Line Drawing
by Bob Amundsen, Buffalo, Wyoming, that
appeared in The Sentry of July 2002.

In the Johnson County jail, Booth's legs were fit with iron shackles, made and riveted on by the town blacksmith. He then began a series of three escape attempts. They each failed but were clever and well thought out. His first attempt was quite unique. Booth kept asking for paper, pen, and ink and then more of the steel nibs used in the pens at that time. What he was doing was tempering them with a candle and urine to a hardness and shape that he was able to "file" through the rivets holding his ankles. A fellow prisoner informed Sheriff Canton as to Booth's plot and that was the end of it. The shackles were again riveted in place. A second attempt involved a different fellow prisoner and work time outside the jailhouse.

They slipped away from the work area when no one was pay-ing attention and then hid in a space between the top of the jail cells and the building roof. When Canton discovered them this time, Booth resisted and was knocked out by a blow to his head by Canton's six-shooter. The third and final attempt was in January 1886. Canton found a rather sizeable hole in Booth's cell floor. Booth had fashioned a make-shift saw by nicking one side of a steel support from within the sole of his boot. Too bad the man did not put all that ingenuity and knowledge to better purpose.

Booth wrote a poignant poem while waiting for the hangman. It was long and rambling; about half of it is transcribed in the following, including all of his spelling, capitalization, and punc-tuation errors.

Air of the Cottage by the Sea

Now come all that I may tell you
far and near from every place.
I am not in no condition for to
Tell you what I know.

For a man can never live long
In the jale at Buffalo.
When I came to Johnson County
I was honest straight & free.
But there is a bad Misfortune that
Has happened unto Me.
It was when I lest expected
That a Man of lowe degree
Hes the cause of all this trouble
That has happened to me.
I have got a wealthy father but
I will not let him know
That I am I this condition
In a jale at Buffalo.
I will never be a freeman so
The truth to you Ile tell
I am now a prisoner in
A Dark and Dreary cel.

Come and lis to what I tell you.
Never leave your Dear old home.
For now I am very sory that
I ever began to roam.
I left home quite a young lad but
I thought that I knew well.
But then now I an A prisoner
In a Dark and Dreary cel.
I have got a dear old father
That I long once more to see.
But a Man in my condition that
Can never never bee.
I have got a Dear old mother
In some low and secret place.
But I never more shall see her
Until Death has takeing place.
Before I cam to this country
I had friends and more than one
But now I have got in trouble
So you see I have none.
Now my days are shortly numbered
But I want you all to see
That a better hearted fellow
In a Jale will never be.

Hon. Bill Booth, Buffalo, Johnson County, Wyoming

A gallows that was ten feet square and had 13 steps leading up to a platform with a lever-controlled trapdoor was built behind the present-day courthouse. Sheriff Canton served as hangman. Booth's last statements were "What time is it?" When told it was 11 am, he replied, "I wish you'd hurry up. I want to get to hell in time for dinner." Twelve minutes later, John Owens aka Bill Booth, departed this life and made his dinner appointment.

Booth's poem was found among the papers in the sheriff's office years after the hanging and published on March 25, 1891, in the Buffalo Bulletin, *page 2, under the caption: "Posthumous Poetry." It was reprinted subsequently in the Gatchell Museum Association's newsletter,* The Sentry, *July 2002.*

Buffalo's First Landlady – 1884
Major Verling K. Hart (1838-1883) filed a Desert Land Entry claim adjacent to
Fort McKinney where the Buffalo community was sited. On his death his wife,
Juliet Watson Hart (b. 1848) was awarded his claim in 1884; she then owned
all of the property in that developing community.

Source: Occidental Hotel and Museum collection

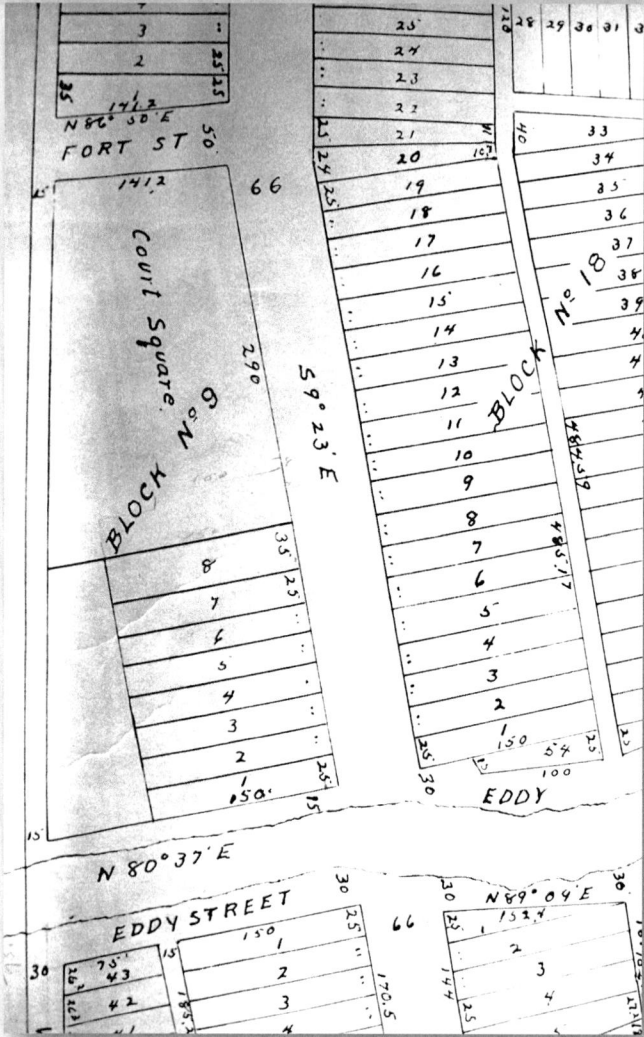

Buffalo's City Plat Map and Land Abstract – 1884
Lower: Portion of original 1884 Buffalo Plat Map developed by Juliet Hart's
surveyors. The irregular lines across the lower portion represent Clear Creek.
The Occidental property was the several lots in Block No. 9 closest to that
stream. Upper: Portion of the Johnson County Land Abstracts for 1884 listing
the Hart to McCray and Buell land sale.

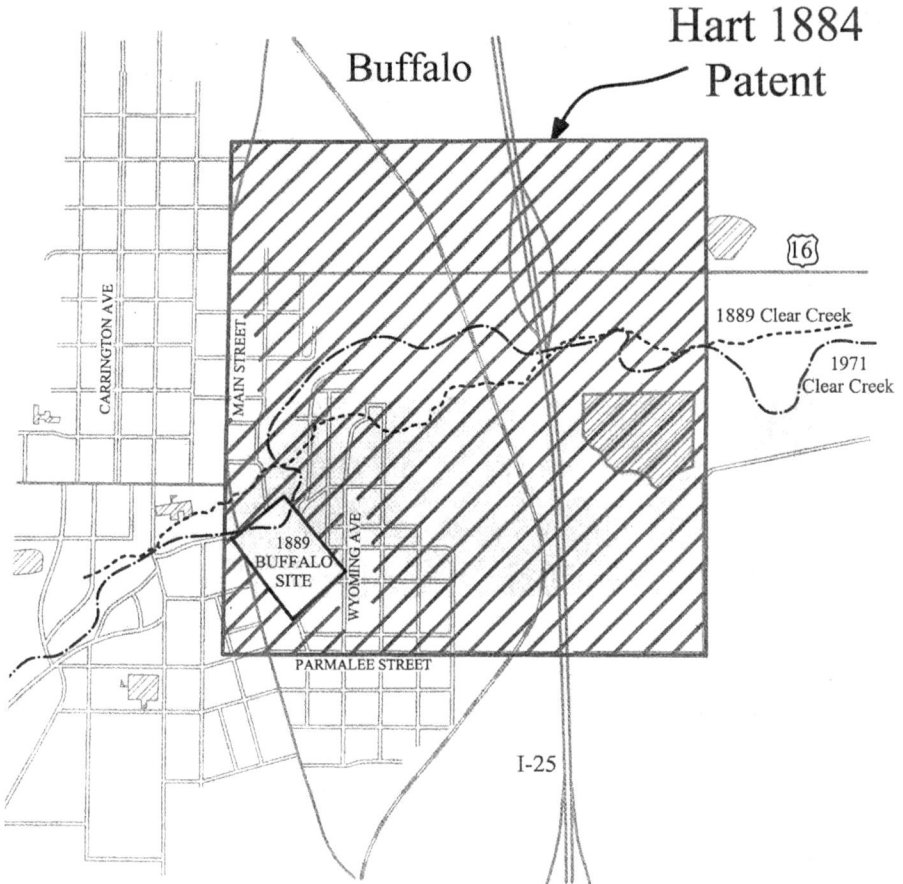

1884 Hart Patent, 1889 Buffalo Site and
1889 Clear Creek on 1971 Map of Buffalo

The Hart Patent and the Town of Buffalo
Depicted here is a superposition of the 1884 Hart Patent and the 1889 Buffalo
town site on a 1971 street map of Buffalo.

Source: Author's collection

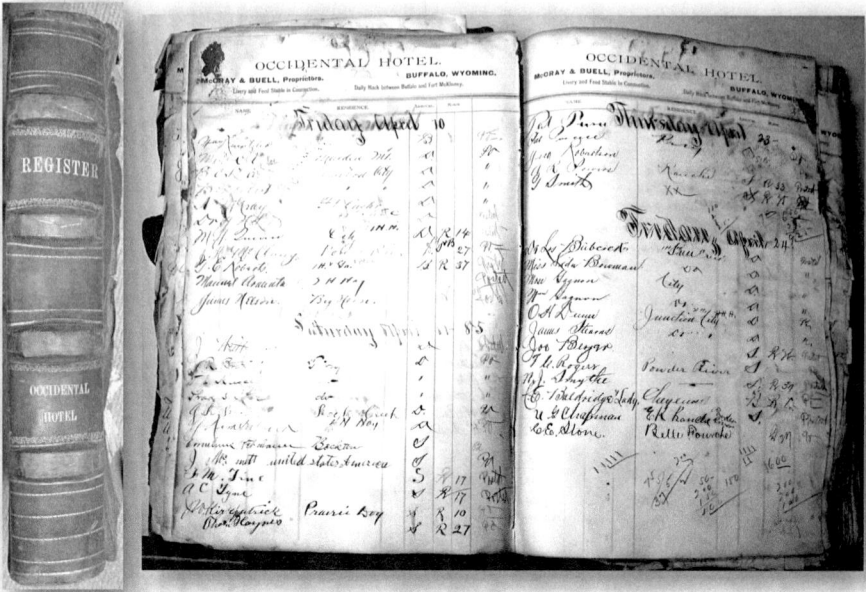

Occidental Guest Register – 1885

Shown above are the spine and two pages from the March-December, 1885
guest register. This is the earliest Guest Register found. The left page is for
April 10 and 11; the right page for April 23 and 24. The intervening pages have
been torn out.

Source: American Heritage Center, University of Wyoming

Occidental Guest Register – 1885

A portion of the guest register page for February 22, 1885 is pictured here;
there were six guests at the hotel on that date. Note that the page heading
informs: "Livery and Feed Stable in Connection" and "Daily Hack between
Buffalo and Fort McKinney."

Source: American
Heritage Center,
University of
Wyoming

Murray Hill Hotel Advertisement
This advertisement appeared in the *Big Horn Sentinel* of November 7, 1885.

Source: Author's collection

Occidental Hotel Trade Tokens
Upper Left: Token for one drink at the Occidental Bar. McCray & Buell era was 1881-1888. A pool table is shown. Upper Right: Five-cent token for the Occidental Bar. This token is reported to be from Buffalo but its origin is questionable. Lower Right: A 12-1/2-cent token while Thomas G. Smith was proprietor (1895-1899). That amount is one-eighth of a dollar and was called a "bit"; two-bits were a quarter, four-bits 50 cents, etc.

Trade tokens are coin-like objects that were used in the frontier West instead of coins from the 17th to the early 19th century because of the acute shortage of government-minted coins. Tokens were a pledge by the merchant to be redeemable in goods at his business. Their sizes, shapes, and materials were widely variable. The collecting of tokens is part of an activity called exonumia.

Source: Johnson County Library (Modified after Bowker and Lenger, 1999)

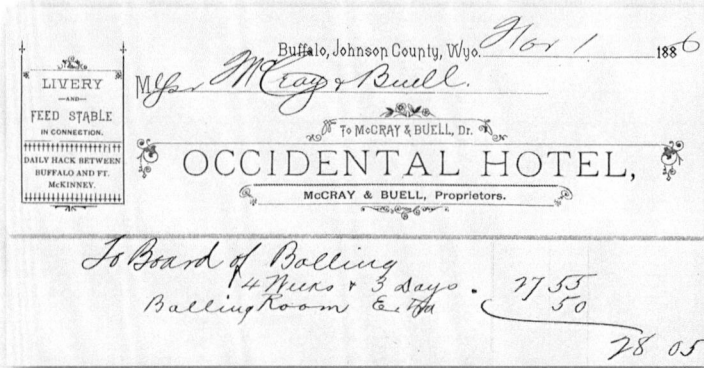

Occidental Invoice – 1886

It is unclear what is being billed by this invoice for $28.05, dated November 1, 1886. The boarding of "Bolling" is 90-cents per day plus an extra 50-cents. Perhaps it is a feed bill?

Source: Johnson County Library

Main Street Parade – mid 1880s

The Buffalo Municipal Band, referred to as "Pap Myers' Band," marching down Main Street in front of the Occidental. The two annex structures adjoining the log hotel are shown clearly in this view. The occasion is probably the 4th of July. Pap Myers, a Bavarian native, was a musician of exceptional ability and associated with all of the early community bands.

Source: Occidental Hotel and Museum collection

Occidental Sign Change
These two photographs show that the Occidental sign has been moved from the original log structure to the large annex.

Presumably, this signifies a move of the main hotel operations to the newer structure. The date of this change is unknown.

Source: Occidental Hotel and Museum collection

Buffalo and the Occidental Hotel – Late 1880s
This panorama of Buffalo, taken about a decade after Buell built his hotel, depicts the Big Horn Mountains on the horizon with Buffalo and Clear Creek in the foreground. The Occidental annex is shown immediately to the right of the Main Street Bridge with the courthouse against the photograph's right edge and the school behind it, to the left.

Source: Occidental Hotel and Museum collection

Clear Creek and the Occidental Hotel – 1900
This photograph, taken a few years later than the preceding one, presents an excellent close-up of Clear Creek and its bridge next to the Occidental Hotel.

Source: Jim Dillinger collection

From Logs to Bricks – 1889-1916

The years following McCray's taking complete control of the Occidental were characterized by a series of ownership changes. There were a total of seven owners and part-owners – McCray, Hathaway, Rinebarger, Beer, Quick, Gilkey, and Waegele – and at least four managers or lease operators – Smith, Quick, Frame, and Angus. The dates and the reasons for each of these changes are unknown.[15] The principal state events during this period were the 1890 admission of Wyoming into the Union as the 44th state and the 1892 Cattle War or Invasion that has received much literary attention. As historically significant and locally traumatic as that episode was, it apparently had no direct adverse effect on the operations of the hotel. It is also difficult to assess the effects from world-wide, economic events of the times – the Depression (1893-1897), the Spanish American War (1898), and World War I (1914-1918) – on a remote Wyoming county. The Depression would be expected to cause everyone to reduce spending as money became scarce while the wars might cause a temporary business pick up. However, given the steady market requirements from the surrounding ranches and adjacent Fort McKinney, Buffalo was growing during the late 1880s to early 1900s time period, thereby providing a stable economic base for the hotel. The Occidental had enough business to keep it in operation so the reasons for the ownership changes was not lack of income but perhaps caused by poor financial management or family/health matters for the owners.

Since the dates and reasons for the individual ownership changes are not known, perhaps the best procedure is to simply list chronologically what can be gleaned from the literature concerning the Occidental from 1889 through 1905 and then for the 1906-1916 period, the first decade in its new brick building. Additional details found in Buffalo newspapers concerning the hotel are included to provide some sense of hotel operations as well as a referral to its changing name and changing proprietors. That listing follows:[16]

1890 McCray advertised in the *Buffalo Echo* that the Occidental was the largest and best hotel in Northern Wyoming with rooms at $2.40 per day and meals served at all hours.

1891 May 28 – Hathaway and Rinebarger complete arrangements to buy the Occidental bar and its billiard parlor. (*Buffalo Bulletin*)

June 11 – Advertisement in the *Buffalo Bulletin* listed W. E. Hathaway and Emory Rinebarger as Occidental proprietors.

June 29 – McCray sold Occidental to Wm. E. Hathaway (*Buffalo Bulletin, July* 9) who changed the name to Burlington, hoping to gain favor with the railroad expected to come into Buffalo. (Buell, 1984, dates the hotel sale as June 1890.)

Aug. – Name change in *Buffalo Bulletin* advertisements from Occidental (August 20th) to Burlington (August 27th).

1892 Sept. 22 – Hathaways sold the Burlington Hotel to Bernard Beer from North Platte, Nebraska, for $10,000; said to be "The largest real estate transaction that has yet taken place in Buffalo, ..." *(Buffalo Bulletin)*

Note: Some newspapers spelled Beer's name with an "e" on the end; the county records do not.

1893 June 8 – *Buffalo Bulletin* article: Hathaway gave up his lease of the Burlington Hotel during the previous week to Bernard Beer. Ex-sheriff Angus then leased the hotel operation and restored the name of Occidental.

Note: The preceding two entries appear to contradict each other – 1892 Hathaway sale to Beer and 1893 Hathaway lease transfer to Beer. However, Beer was an absentee owner, i.e., he did not operate the hotel himself. Apparently, after the September 1892 sale, Hathaway continued to operate the hotel on a lease basis until June of the following year.

Nov. 12 – William G. Angus – Andrew S. Brown shooting outside Occidental; Angus subsequently found guilty of aggravated assault and battery; fined $250 plus $100 costs. (*Buffalo Bulletin*, Nov. 14)

1894 *Buffalo Bulletin* advertisements: A. A. Frame, manager, "Burlington Hotel formerly Occidental."

1895 May 18 – *Buffalo Bulletin* advertisement for the Occidental lists Thomas G. Smith, proprietor. An interesting note: C. E. Buell is reported to be the proprietor of a new Occidental Hotel in Sheridan.

Note: A synonym for proprietor is "owner" but the word can also mean, "one having an interest (as control or present use) less than an absolute or exclusive right." The *Buffalo Bulletin* uses the term in both ways – owner or operator – and simply does not draw a distinction. In this case, T. G. Smith holds a lease and not ownership as stated in their November 4, 1899 issue.

July 30 – Hotel damaged by Clear Creek flood; water poured through the dining room and carried away some tables and chairs. Adjacent wooden building that served as city hall was swept away and all city records were lost.

Sept. 28 – Another ad for the Occidental with Smith as proprietor. *(Buffalo Bulletin)*

1896 Tom Smith and brother, Harry (Henry A.) operate the hotel; name changed back to Occidental; Red Angus ran the bar. February 8th and November 21st Occidental advertisements listed T. Smith as proprietor. *(People's Voice)* [17]

Aug. 31 – Killing of Hugh Smith by Z. M. French, Occidental Hotel Manager. *(Buffalo Bulletin, Sept. 3)*

Dec. 12 – T. G. Smith leases kitchen-dining room to James M. Karns. *(People's Voice)*

1897 Jan. 16 – T. G. Smith resumed duties in kitchen-dining room. *(People's Voice)*

July 3 – T. G. Smith has new sidewalk installed in front of hotel. *(People's Voice)*

Aug. 7 – Telegraph branch office opened in Occidental with Sam McDonald, operator. *(People's Voice)*

Nov. 27 – T. G. Smith plans new brick addition between present office and dining room. The new addition will include an office, barber shop, and bath rooms; the barroom to be extended and upgraded. *(People's Voice)*

1898 Dec. 17 – More alterations planned for the Occidental. (*Buffalo Voice*)

July 9 – Colorado Dispensary physicians, specialists in chronic diseases, at Occidental – consultations free. (*Buffalo Voice*)

Note: An ongoing series of visits by medical, dental, and vision specialists developed in Buffalo. They tend to use the Occidental as their offices while in town. A few made outrageous claims in local newspapers but the majority did not.

Mar. 19 – Dr. W. O. Owen at Occidental for two weeks (specialty not given).

1899 Jan. 21 – Occidental wired for 62 electric lights. (*Buffalo Voice*)

May 13 – The Sheridan Steam Laundry made arrangements for daily pickup and delivery of clothes at the Occidental. (*Buffalo Voice*)

Sept. 2 – "Bernard Beer of Denver, the owner of the Occidental hotel in this city, arrived Tuesday evening and went south to his ranch the next morning." (*Buffalo Voice*)

Oct. 28 – T. G. Smith renovating Occidental: rooms for a barber shop, washroom and bathroom to be added between the office and barroom. (*Buffalo Voice*)

Nov. 4 – T. G. Smith sold his lease and the fixtures, etc. of the Occidental to O. N. Quick. (*Buffalo Voice*)

1900 Jan. 6 – Occidental advertisement lists O. N. Quick as proprietor but he holds a lease and is not the owner.

Mar. 3 – Bernard Beer, Occidental owner, in town from Denver. (*Buffalo Voice*)

May 5 – Dr. Donohue, Osteopath, Omaha, in Occidental for June and July. (*Buffalo Voice*)

Oct. 6 – Fred Clausen resumed position as the hotel's bartender. (*Buffalo Voice*)

Oct. 13 – Registry Agents meet in Occidental. (*Buffalo Voice*)

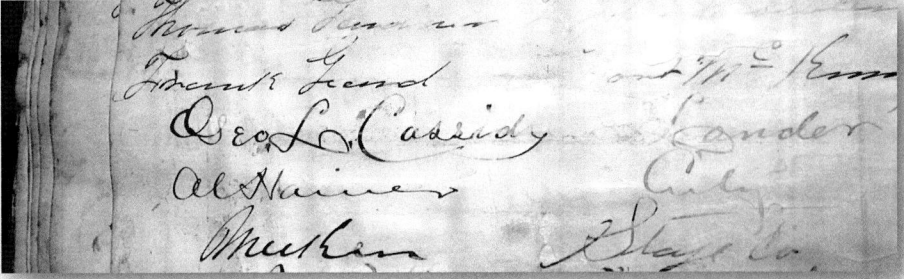

**Butch Cassidy Registration at
the Occidental Hotel – 1890**

Robert LeRoy Parker (1866-1908) was a notorious train and bank robber and leader of the Wild Bunch gang. His principal alias was Butch Cassidy but he used several different ones including the George L. Cassidy on the Occidental Register for November 15, 1890 (lower). It is interesting that he wrote Lander for his residence. His picture here was cropped from a copy of the well known photograph of the Wild Bunch taken in Texas in 1901. The signatures above and below Cassidy's – Frank Grouard and Al Hainer, respectively also appear to be authentic. The Fort McKinney residence for Grouard is correct and for Hainer it appears to be Cody or City. All three individuals were known to have been in the area on the 1890 date.

Source: Author's collection and (Signatures) American Heritage Center, University of Wyoming

1901 Jan. 5 – Fort McKinney's Company C held their 10th annual Drill and Ball at the Armory followed by an 11 p.m. dinner at the Occidental. *(Buffalo Voice)*

Aug. 8 – Governor Richards visits Buffalo and the Occidental. *(Buffalo Bulletin)*

Aug. 22 – A valuable watch was stolen from a guest at the Occidental. The thief was caught and confessed. While waiting for the next session of court to be sentenced, he was confined in the local jail. He managed to escape by filing through two of the bars at his window, took the absent jailer's rifle, and escaped. No follow-up information was found. *(Buffalo Bulletin)*

1902 Stockgrowers Bank of Buffalo organized this year; it plans to occupy the new North Annex of Occidental when constructed.

1903 Mar. 26 – Oscar Quick acquired half-interest with option to purchase the other half (*Buffalo Bulletin,* Apr. 2); O. A. Gilkey deeded one-quarter interest. Brick addition to the Occidental completed.

1905 May 19 – Quick and Gilkey now have complete ownership; changed to Quick and Waegele: May 31st One-third interest deeded to Fred Waegele. (Not noted in liquor license application – see following.)

May 31 – O. N. Quick & Co. (O. N. Quick and O. A. Gilkey) make annual application to Johnson County for Occidental's liquor license. (*Buffalo Voice,* June 3)

Sept. 9 – New hotel and bank building to be erected; 34×70 ft., two stories, brick construction, sited just north of present Occidental building, Stockgrowers Bank to occupy front 50 ft of lower floor. Occidental owners O. N. Quick, O. A. Gilkey and Fred Waegele, let a construction contract to C. M. Culp for approximately $14,750; second floor to contain 20 rooms plus bathrooms and a parlor; steam heat. (*Buffalo Voice*). Nearing completion – to be ready about middle January. (*Buffalo Voice,* December 30)

The Occidental Hotel and the 1892 Johnson County War

The 1892 war was a protracted series of conflicts in Johnson County between large ranchers on one side and homesteaders and small ranchers on the other. At issue was the control and use of open range grasslands. There were five killings and two lynchings before, during, and after the climactic "Invasion" by the Wyoming Stock Growers Association members and their hired Texas gunmen. It was a true county-level civil war that pitted neighbor against neighbor but also involved governmental officials at the state and national levels. Much has been written about this major frontier era event. The earliest account was *Banditti of the Plains* by Asa Mercer in 1892, now a true classic, and the most recent are *The Johnson County War* by Bill O'Neal in 2004 and John Davis' *Wyoming Range War* in 2010. Both authors present complete and unbiased accounts; O'Neal adds new information on the hired Texan gunmen and Davis provides the analyses of a lawyer.

It is somewhat surprising that the Occidental Hotel is rarely mentioned in the extant literature on this major event in western history. As *the* local meeting place, there is little doubt that the hotel did house many discussions, meetings, etc., of local residents during the entire conflict but none of them made the historians' accounts. The only Buffalo business that is mentioned prominently is Robert Foote's general merchandise store that he threw open to outfit the Buffalo defenders with guns, ammunition, and supplies – all gratis.

Burlington Hotel Forms – Early 1890s
During the early 1890s, the Hathaway owners changed the Occidental's name to the Burlington Hotel in anticipation of that railroad building a line into Buffalo. Upper: Hotel letterhead stationery. Lower: An Invoice, dated Jan. 1st, 1892; its contents are unclear.

Source: Lower: Modified after Buell, Helen, 1984
Upper: American Heritage Center, University of Wyoming

Sunday, June. 17, 1900.

T. O. Hill — City
P. Healy Jr — "
Cook — Ranch
Holstine — City
S. C. Hunt
Mrs Hunt
Arthur Smith
Frank Rollins
Jessie Emison
Fay Martin
W. H. Bittner
Ella Bittner
Geo Lathrop
Edw. J. Fischer
C. H. Hill

THE BITTNER THEATRE ARMORY HALL
com. Monday June 18th
with What Happened to Smith

OCCIDENTAL HOTEL.
A. J. McCRAY, PROPRIETOR. BUFFALO, WYO.
Livery and Feed Stable in Connection.

NAME	RESIDENCE	Arrival	Room
W. McP Fuller Omaha Representing Blake Bruce and Co Druggists			
Geo Mitchell Omaha Representing W H Page and Co Soap Mangs			
J T Spivey Omaha Representing Farrell and Co Syrup Mangs			
S D Blythe Sioux City Representing Sioux Cracker Co And Candy Mangs			
A B Browne Chicago Representing H C Fisher Importe and Jobber of Teas and Cigars			

Arrived June 8th 1891
Per Special Team
Dusty Drummers

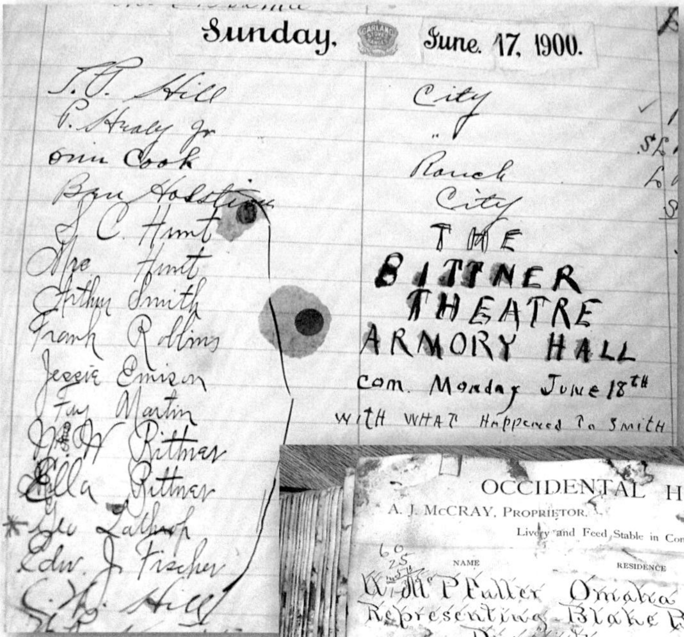

Traveling Entertainment Groups at the Occidental Hotel

These Occidental guest register pages list two entertainment groups – The Dusty Drummers, 1891, and the Bittner Theatre Group, 1900. It was typical for such groups to stay at the hotel where some of their performances were conducted.

Source: American Heritage Center, University of Wyoming

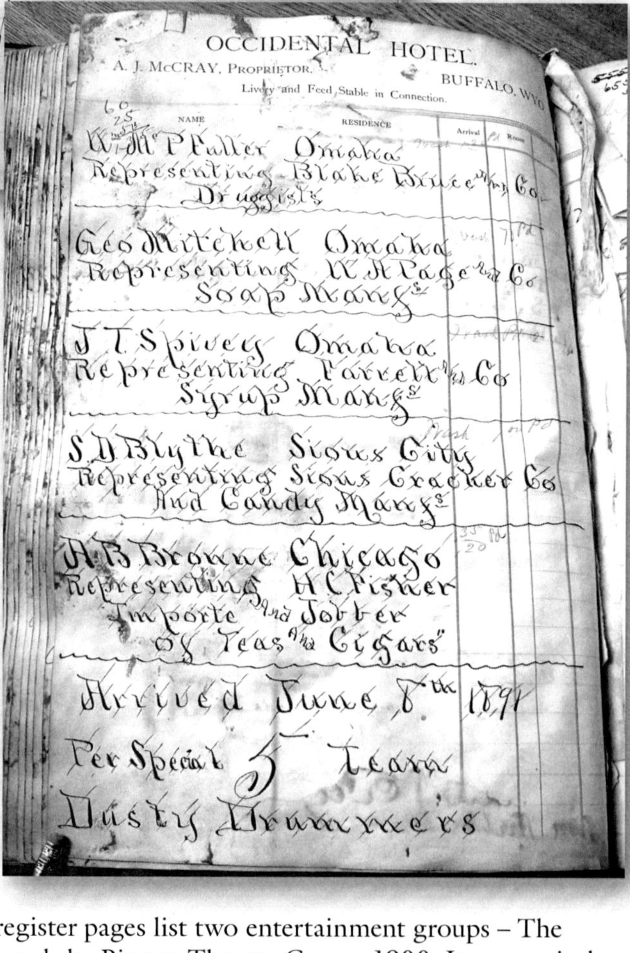

Western Union Telegraph Key
This key was a gift from the Smith family to the Wexos and is currently on display at the Occidental Hotel. It is said to have been from a Western Union office in the Occidental tavern and used during the 1892 Cattle War. It appears to be a Western Union 15B Steel Sounder on a wooden base with a Straight Telegraph Key. The two cylindrical electromagnets provide the necessary current to make a loud "clack" when the key is depressed.

Source: Author's collection

Notice of Occidental Sale
This notice appeared in the *Buffalo Bulletin* of September 22, 1892, and records the Hathaway to Beer sale of the Occidental for $10,000.

Source: Author's collection

Signs of the Times.

The largest real estate transaction that has yet taken place in Buffalo, was completed to-day in the office of Mr. Charles H. Burritt Mr. Bernard Beer of North Platte, Nebraska, purchased from Mr. and Mrs. William E. Hathaway, the property known as the Burlington Hotel, together with all the lots, appurtenant thereto. The property in question, which forms one of the most desirable locations in the very centre of the business quarter of Buffalo, is described as follows: Lots 1, 2, 3, 4, 5, 12, 13, 14, 15, 16, south 13 feet, lot 6, and 613 feet, lot 11 in block 9.

The consideration was $10,000. Mr. Beer may be congratulated on obtaining this property, which is exactly suited to the requirements of a first-class hotel, and this unmistakable sign of the growing prosperity of Buffalo will be welcomed by all. This is only the beginning of the boom.

The folklore associated with one of the Occidental's antique items, however, tells of a very direct involvement between the Invaders and the Occidental. That item is an antique telegraph key donated by the Smith Family during the Occidental restoration. Telegraph key is a general term used for any switching device used to send signals, primarily Morse Code, by manual telegraphy. The Occidental key is said to have been the one used by Western Union during the time that agency had an office in the hotel. The story of its connection with the Johnson County Cattle War is as follows:

> When the Invaders saw that they were surrounded by a large posse and could not leave the TA Ranch, they needed to get word of their situation to support- ers in Buffalo at the Occidental Hotel. One of their group knew telegraphy and how to tap into a line for transmission. He managed to reach a telegraph line and sent a message to the Occidental Western Union office that was received by the key which the hotel still has on display. That successfully contacted the Invaders' supporters but also informed any of their opponents who happened to be present.

The Johnson County Cattle War literature tells of the surrounded Invaders contact with the outside in an entirely different manner. It makes no mention of any contact with the Occidental. The details of how the besieged cattlemen and gunfighters got word of their plight at the TA to Cheyenne with an appeal for help are skimpy and unclear. One account has it that an Invader managed to make his way through the defender lines, got to an open telegraph line and contacted Cheyenne (did he also contact the Occidental?). Another explanation is that while the telegraph lines south of Buffalo were kept down most of the time, the line north from Fort McKinney was not cut. Local friends of the Invaders were able to use that line to eventually get through to Cheyenne by an alternate transmission line routing.

Thus, we are left with the situation where the folklore associated with an antique item finds no direct support in the literature of the period. It is, however, useful to keep in mind that folklore has its proper place in history as the written record does not contain all events of interest. A favorite quote of the author's is "Oral traditions supply invaluable, if not infallible, information."

Shoot-Outs at the Old Occidental

How many shootings actually occurred in the Occidental is not known. During the recent renovation in the early 1990s, more than twenty bullet holes were found in the saloon's walls and ceilings! Their exact sources and times are, of course, not known; several were left unchanged for the visual record. The preceding chronology lists the two instances of gunplay that have been recorded: Angus-Brown in 1893 and French-Smith in 1896. Bullets found their mark in both cases with a most unusual injury for Brown and fatality for Smith.

William Galispie "Red" Angus (1849-1922) and Andrew "Arapaho" Brown (1844-1901) were two of Buffalo's important frontier characters. Angus brought a herd of cattle from the Pacific Northwest into Johnson County in 1880 and spent the remainder of his life there. His nickname derived from his red hair and fierce temper. Angus initially engaged in the saloon business and prostitution with their ready markets from the soldiers at nearby Fort McKinney. His involvement in those activities was not forgotten – when Laurel Avenue, Buffalo's frontier red light area, was renamed in the 1950s; it became Angus Street.

Over time, however, Angus dealt with the law on both sides: being arrested (1881 and 1884) and making arrests as Johnson County Sheriff for two terms (1889-1893). He is perhaps best known for being the county sheriff during the 1892 Johnson County Cattle War or Invasion. In 1893, after his last term as sheriff, Angus leased the Occidental saloon and returned to bartending.[18]

Andrew Stalnaker "Arapaho" Brown was definitely a colorful character, even unsavory, as there always seemed to be stories and suspicions of wrongdoing connected with him. He has been described as a large, powerful man – over six feet tall and 275 pounds with an aggressive attitude. Brown served in Company E, West Virginia Volunteers, during the Civil War after which he came to Wyoming. He is said to have lived with the Arapaho Indians for a number of years as a trader and learned to speak their difficult, guttural language. This was the source of his nickname which was usually shortened to "Rap." He was active in a leadership role during Buffalo's response to the Invaders. Sheriff Angus was investigating at the KC cabin where Champion and Ray had been killed the previous day so Brown took charge of forming and leading a posse to confront the Invaders barricaded at the TA Ranch south of town.[19]

William "Red" Angus (upper) and Andrew "Arapaho" Brown
Sources: Upper – Johnson County Library collection
Lower – Jim Gatchell Memorial Museum collection.
Signatures: American Heritage Center, University of Wyoming

Following is the description of the Angus-Brown gunfight as published in the *Buffalo Bulletin* on November 14, 1893:

> On Sunday evening [Nov. 10] about 8:30 a shooting scrape took place outside the Occidental. It appears that a quarrel arose between W. G. Angus and Arapahoe [sic] Brown over an old account. Brown called at the Occidental hotel several times during the day, but Angus was not to be seen. In the evening he came in and called Angus out into the street. The latter who had probably learned of Mr. Brown's intentions, armed himself with a 32 caliber pistol and went out. Just what passed is not easy to learn, but Tom Smith and Wm. Miller who followed him out anticipating trouble, were just in time to see one shot fired by Angus. They immediately caught hold of him and a second shot that he fired went wide. Brown who was hit by the first shot walked up to Dr. Gossett's room and Angus was

arrested by the City Marshal. The whole business took place so quickly that by time a crowd had collected both parties had disappeared. On examination it was found that the bullet had gone through Brown's overcoat, vest and two shirts, glanced off the collar bone and lodged somewhere in the upper part of the chest. Dr. Gossett extracted a piece of woolen shirt from the wound but could not exactly locate the ball. Mr. Brown was walking around Monday rather sore, but apparently little the worse for his adventure. Which party was to blame is at present a matter of conjecture only. Brown has a reputation as a thumper, but if he really made the threats attributed to him he could scarcely complain that they were taken seriously. But for Tom Smith and Wm. Miller he would probably have had a very small chance of explaining his intentions as he was unarmed.

District Court Docket Items for the William "Red" Angus Trial
The docket folder cover (left) and jury verdict (right) for the trial of the November 12, 1893 shooting of Andrew "Arapaho" Brown outside the Occidental Hotel. In addition to the verdict sheet, the docket folder held all of the trial records.   Source: Author's collection

Angus was arrested, tried, and convicted. Even though it was determined that Brown was unarmed, the jury recommended leniency for Angus, and his charge was reduced to aggravated assault and battery. He was fined $250 plus $100 costs – Brown had to have been surprised to learn that his trauma was worth so little. Angus returned to bartending and then, from 1909 to retirement in 1920, he served as county clerk, county treasurer, and Commandant at the Soldiers and Sailors Home on the old Fort McKinney site. This complex man, with an extremely varied career, died peacefully in his sleep at age 70 years in 1922.[20]

Brown continued to carry the Angus .32 caliber lead bullet somewhere in his chest cavity for the following several years with no apparent ill effect. His relationships with other individuals, however, did not improve. In 1901, Brown was shot again and this time the result was fatal. On investigation by Sheriff Kennedy only his remains – bones and buttons – were found in the ashes of his own ranch woodpile. Reportedly, they were buried in a child's coffin. Brown's two murderers were caught and they confessed. Both men pleaded guilty to second degree murder and were given life sentences.[21]

Red Angus and Andrew Brown are both buried in Buffalo's Willow Grove Cemetery and continue to rest there to the present day.

The second recorded Occidental shooting occurred three years later on August 31, 1896. The killer was Z. M. French, the hotel's manager at the time, and the victim was Hugh C. Smith, an ex-employee of the Occidental who had maintained residence there. The exchange of gunfire between the two men was caused by a domestic quarrel that involved Mrs. French, the manager's wife and hotel headwaiter, and Smith. That quarrel in the hotel kitchen developed into physical contact – battery – between the two individuals. Peter McGinnis, having dinner at the hotel, heard noise in the kitchen, went there, and saw Smith kicking Mrs. French who was on the floor. McGinnis then went to French's office and told him what he had just seen. French took his revolver, a .45 caliber Colt, and went to the kitchen. Gunfire was exchanged. Smith missed French but was himself shot three times – in the hip, abdomen, and spine. Smith had fired his .38 caliber revolver only once. Smith lived about eight hours before dying of his wounds.

Arapaho Brown's
Undertaker and Funeral

A rather detailed biography of Brown was published by Thelma Gatchell Condit in 1966. Written in an anecdotal style, it portrays him as a complicated man – as given to violence with his fellow man as to writing poetry for a girl he was courting. Condit's description of how Brown's remains, bones and buttons, were dealt with after being brought to Buffalo by Sheriff Kennedy is unusual and interesting enough to warrant quoting here:

> *Old Rap's bones caused a lot of excitement in town. J. A. Jones was undertaker at the time. Flatrock Jones he was called, because he was tight with his money. He was short, rather heavy set man with a big mustache. He ran a saloon [on Main Street], not a fancy saloon like Zindle's up the street; just a common, run-of-the-mill place where the drunkest drunks held sway. Flatrock had his 'funeral parlor' in the rear of the saloon. This served more than one purpose, for whenever a man got too inebriated, all Flatrock had to do was lead him into the back room and leave him alone a minute or two. Upon finding himself surrounded by coffins, and once in a while one with a corpse in it, he immediately remembered he had rushing business to be attended to elsewhere, anywhere in fact, but here, and he usually departed 'dead sober', too. This was an ideal setup for Jones for he could handle two businesses himself this way...*

> *Flatrock had Rap's bones lying in state in the funeral parlor back of the saloon. Everybody for miles around had to come in and look at them. Flatrock had a really thriving saloon business, for nearly every man had to fortify himself with a little snort in order to sort of calm himself down and talk about the murder sensibly. It was kind of a spooky subject, the more one thought about it.*

> *One old-timer told me, "In those days, by gum, a kid just didn't get in a saloon, but Old Flatrock let me and some other boys in to see Rap's bones. Had 'em in a baby casket. We was plumb flabbergasted to think them bones was all that was left of big old Rap Brown. I'll never forget the coffins stacked on the sides of the room. Didn't take us kids long to see what we wanted to see."* [22]

Occidental Bullet Holes
Three of the bullet holes found in the walls of the Occidental are shown above.
They are in the bar room's ceiling (upper) and wall (lower).

Source: Photographs courtesy of John Gavin

A coroner's jury found French guilty, he was charged with manslaughter, and his bond was set at $2,500. The preliminary hearing for this case was held in the Justice of the Peace court on Friday, September 3. The lawyers on either side made no pleas and the case was dismissed on the grounds of self-defense. The general sentiment was that French had adequate cause for shooting upon seeing his wife being beaten; the *Buffalo Bulletin* article on the event included the statement, "French undoubtedly had gross provocation for his actions."[23]

A Pistol Whipping in the Occidental Bar

There is another recorded instance of gunplay in the Occidental but this one involved pistol whipping and not shooting. The combatants were Frank Canton, sheriff, stock detective, and a leader of the cattlemen's 1892 Invasion force and Will Foster, blacklisted by Wyoming Stock Growers Association as a rustler and on its death list. From that time on there was bad blood between the two men and it would climax in 1899. The story of the incident was recalled by J. Elmer Brock, a prominent local rancher, who witnessed it.

Canton had been drinking heavily in the Occidental Bar when he asked Foster to have a drink. Foster declined, heated words were exchanged, Canton said he was going to kill Foster and reached for his gun. Foster, being younger and quicker, beat Canton to the draw. However, instead of shooting Canton, he hit him over the head with his six shooter so hard that it flew out of his hand. Canton did not finish drawing his gun but reached for Foster's gun on the floor. Clearly, he meant to shoot Foster with his own gun. Foster pushed Canton aside, retrieved his gun and proceeded to beat Canton with it. He stopped when he apparently thought Canton was dead. He was not, but some 60 stitches were required to repair the lacerations on his head. After recuperating, Canton and Foster met once again on Buffalo's Main Street and walked past each other on the sidewalk without acknowledging the other's presence. The conflict between the two men was finally over.[24] By early 1901, Canton had left Wyoming and went to Oklahoma.

An Early Morning Visit by the Governor

A visit by the state governor is always a major event in a small community. On August 8, 1901, Governor DeForest Richards (1846-1903) visited Buffalo along with F. Chatterson, Secretary of State, and T. T. Tynan, Superintendent of Public Instruction. A previous telegram to local rancher and businessman, W. J. Thom, had asked that the governor's party be met at the train station in Clearmont and provided transportation to Buffalo. The purpose of the visit was to inspect the two sections (1,280 acres) of military reserve land that had been transferred to the state following the abandonment of Fort McKinney in 1894. Buffalo resolved to give Governor Richards and party *"... an impromptu, but cordial reception, which should testify to their regard both for the man and the office he so worthily fills."* [25]

DRS. GRAY BROTHERS

WILL REMAIN

ONE WEEK LONGER!

——Rooms at——

OCCIDENTAL HOTEL.

Teeth Extracted without pain or harm by means of Vitalized Air.

Teeth filled by Electricity without Pain.

REFERENCES:

Will Refer to Numbers of Buffalo's Best Citizen's.

OCCIDENTAL HOTEL,

Central Location
Oldest and Best.

Tables provided with the best the country affords. Bar supplied with the best Liquors and Cigars.

Every attention given to the comfort of guests.

T. G. Smith, Prop'r.

Old Time Reunion.

Yourself and lady are cordially invited to attend a Ball and Supper, Wednesday Evening, February 11.

Dance at City Hall, 8:30 p. m.

Supper at Occidental Hotel at 11 p. m.

C. W. Round.

Occidental Advertisements

Left: A dentist at the Occidental. This advertisement appeared in the *People's Voice* of June 13, 1896. It is unusual in its exaggerated claims and the fact that most visiting medical specialists only advertised the dates of their availability. Upper right: Routine hotel advertisement. The advertisement appeared in the *People's Voice* of November 6, 1897. It is typical of the hotel's ads. Lower right: Invitation to a reunion dance and dinner. The date and particulars of this invitation are not known.

Sources: Left and Upper right – Author's collection; Lower right – Johnson County Library

All of the preceding was done – transportation provided from Clearmont to Buffalo and a cordial reception. What was so unusual in the otherwise ordinary event was that it occurred between two a.m. and four a.m.! Additionally, the greeting was anything but impromptu.

Famous Occidental Guests

Both Calamity Jane (1852-1903) and William F. Cody (1846-1917) are reputed to have stayed at the Occidental. Dates unknown.

Source: Occidental Hotel and Museum collection

The visitors arrived in Buffalo at two a.m. and were met at the city line by the Buffalo brass band, Company C of the 2nd Regiment, commanded by Captain G. E. A. Moeller. They were then escorted to the Occidental Hotel. A large contingent of Buffalo's leading citizens awaited the governor's party. The list of those 43 attendees in the *Buffalo Bulletin* read like a local who's who and included: W. J. Thom, W. H. Zindel, O. N. Quick, T. J and P. A. Gatchell, G. F. Myers, T. P. Hill, George Munkres, W. P. Keays, J. E. Chappell. A banquet in the Occidental's dining room was followed by a brief address by Senator Wilson McBride and responded to by Governor Richards. The welcoming ended at four a.m. when Company C presented arms to their commander-in-chief who thanked them for the salute and complimented their overall record.

While Buffalo's welcome seems a bit overboard, the question not answered in the newspaper article was "Why so early?" The time

Registered at the Occidental.

Alex. McMeans, Clear creek; George Buell, Rock creek; Frank Cross and Frank Edwards, Jewell, Kan.; J. E. Greub and A. J. Reamer, Kearney; C. M. Devoe and Fred. Lee, Trabing; W. E. Lee, Fremont, Neb.; John Hepp and wife, Crazy Woman; A. W. Ryerson, Detroit, Mich.; Harry Huson, Clearmont; T. J. Gardiner and wife and L. A. Webb and wife, Mayoworth; Thomas Connolly and John Connolly, jr., Box Elder; M: C. Wilcox and brother, Mrs. R. Foote jr., E. D. Metcalf and wife, City; R. F. Bacon, Deadwood, S. D.; A. Tschirgi, E. E. Enterline, J. L. Stotts, E. E. Lonabaugh, J. B. Menardi and J. B. Bethuren, Sheridan; Allen G. Fisher, Chadron, Neb.; Chas. S. Hunting, Lusk; F. A. Jones and family, Greub; Fred. Winningar, Kaycee; James Rinker, Mayoworth; Ben. Holstein, Sheridan; M. B. Camplin, Newcastle; R. L. Taylor, Mayoworth; John Eldredge and wife, Sussex; W. C. Caven, Crawford, Nebr., E. Gardiner, Sheridan; E. J. Latham, Mrs. R. D. Loy, G. M. Ellis, T. F. Carr and A. E. Sutton, Kaycee; Geo. Snelling, Richie Young, R. S. Billings, E. E. Vreeland, Frank Turinck, Henry Uekman and Fred. Barling, T. W. ranch; Zeke Arrington, Clearmont; G. A. Comstock, Alti Pendergraft and J. D. Webb, Griggs; G. A. Blake, A. M. Applegel, O. N. Quick, J. Jonny, Sheridan; Mrs. N. Fay and W. H. Spear, Big Horn; A. E. Pike, St. Jos, Mo.; H. J. Caulfield, Omaha, Neb.; E. A. Smith and George Kaltenbach, Kaycee; Horace Brown, French creek; A. T. Bacon, Denver, Colo.; W. B. Holler, Geiggs; Wm. Bryant and C. E. Buell and family, Rock creek; Geo. Woodael, Sheridan; W. S. Hill, Mayoworth.

List of Occidental Registrants

On an irregular basis, the Buffalo newspapers would publish lists of the names of the individuals registered at the Occidental. Apparently, there was no objection to this practice. The list here is for 80 hotel guests from 18 local and in-state towns and seven different states: Colorado, Kansas, Michigan, Missouri, Montana, Nebraska, and South Dakota. It appeared in the *Buffalo Voice* of May 6, 1899 and is unusually long; most lists were about half as long. Source: Author's collection

Occidental Guest Register – 1904

The top half of the guest register page for September 4, 1904. Source: Author's collection

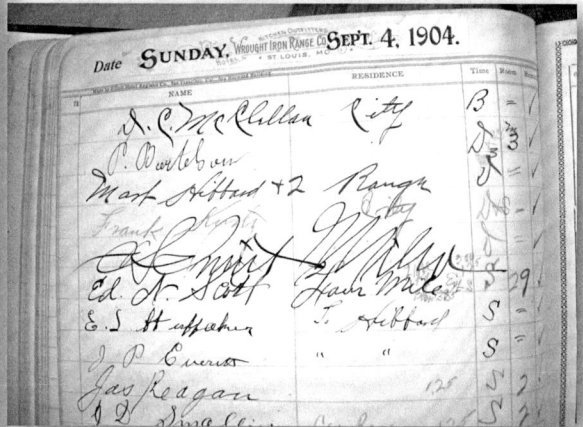

was clearly dictated by the governor and it could be that he expected to simply be taken to the hotel to get some rest. Wonder how long it was before he visited Buffalo again?

As previously noted, the Occidental's owners, Oscar N. Quick and Fred Waegele, had let a contract the preceding September for replacing the old wooden buildings with a new one of brick construction. The 1903 brick addition, two stories and 33 feet wide, was already in place on the north side of the old structure, away from Clear Creek. The old annex buildings were torn down and their logs and lumber hauled away for use on a nearby ranch. The bricks used for the new structure were from a kiln located several miles south of town. Total construction cost $65,000.

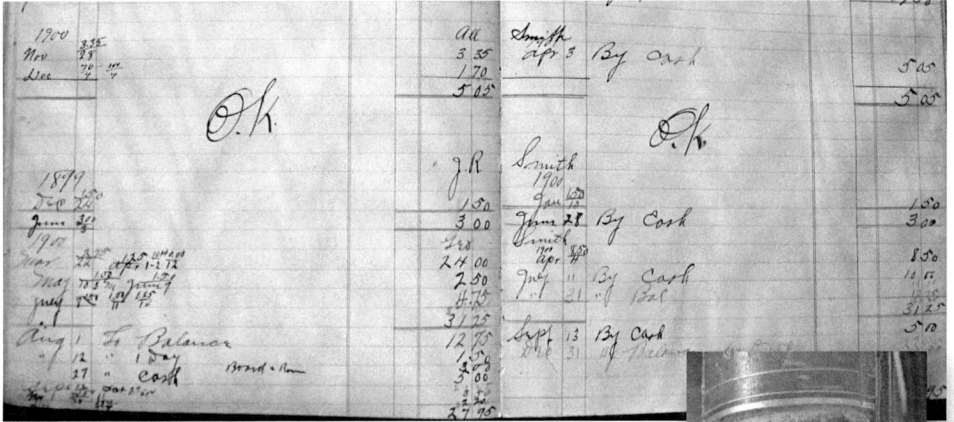

Occidental Transfer Register 1899-1901
The Transfer Register was used to record the
hotel guest's charges and payments. Their
names were transferred from the guest register.
Spaces were provided for the number of people
in each party, the days stayed, meals, extra
purchases, e.g., cigars, fees, and payments.
Shown are the spine and one page from the
1899 Register. The guest names are Al Smith
(top) and J. R. Smith; their stays were from
December 1899 to June 1901.

Source: Author's collection

The new, two-story, brick Occidental was completed in two
phases: a 53-foot wide section in 1908 which included a new saloon,
was next to the 1903 addition; then, in 1910, a 36-foot wide final
section, between it and the Clear Creek bank.[26] The resulting hotel
had a frontage of 122 feet. Open to the public, the first floor of the
new hotel held the lobby, dining room, barbershop, and the new
Occidental bar with its card and billiard rooms. A laundry and sleep-
ing quarters for some of the help were built behind the hotel. For a
community of some 2,000, it was a very impressive structure.[27] An
advertisement in the *Buffalo Bulletin* (December 22, 1910) listed it
as the Occidental Hotel Annex, Warren & Company, Proprietors,
and extolled its steam heat, running hot and cold water, rooms
with bath, up-to-date buffet, barbershop, spacious and convenient
sample room. What more could a traveler possibly want? Warren &
Company probably managed, but did not own the hotel.

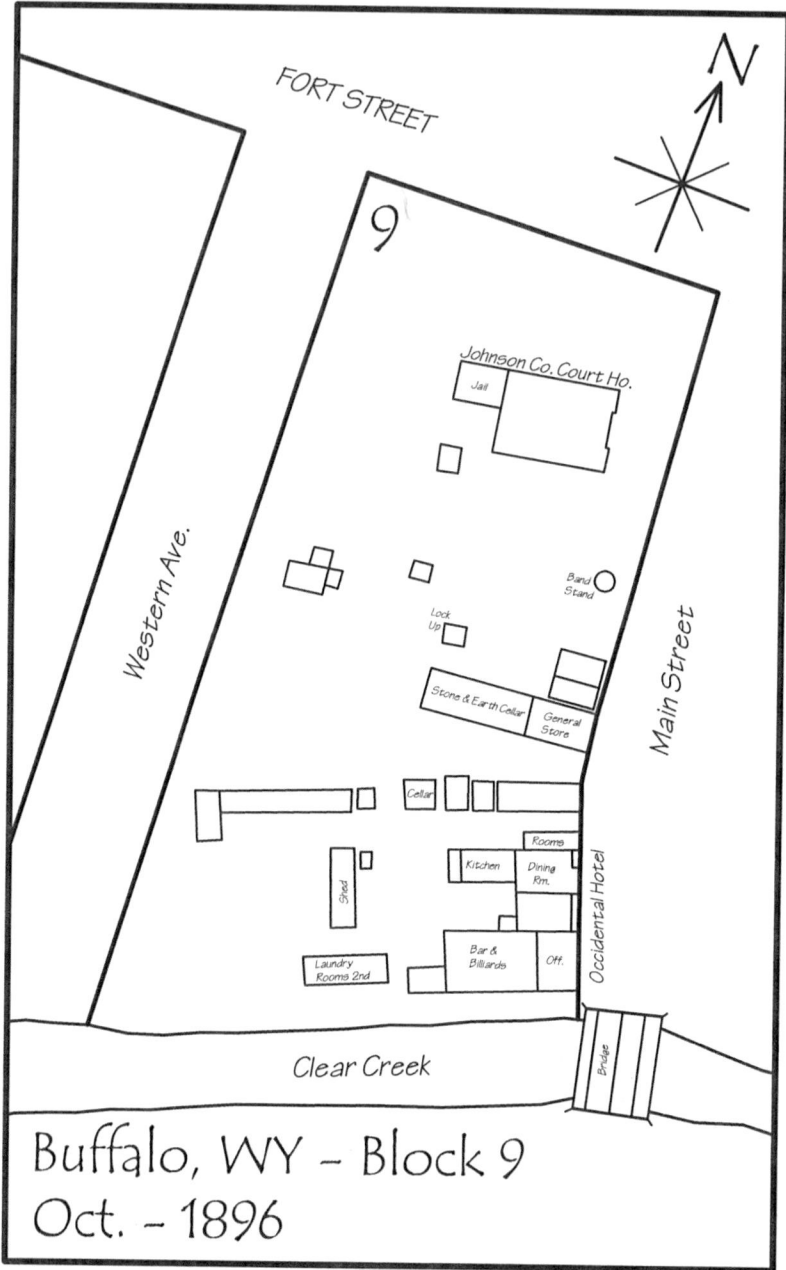

FORT STREET

9

Johnson Co. Court Ho.

Jail

Western Ave.

Band
Stand

Lock
Up

Main Street

Stone & Earth Cellar

General
Store

Cellar

Rooms

Kitchen

Dining
Rm.

Shed

Occidental Hotel

Bar &
Billiards

Off.

Laundry
Rooms 2nd

Bridge

Clear Creek

Buffalo, WY – Block 9
Oct. – 1896

Buffalo Street Plan – 1896
This map shows the west side of the first block of Main Street North that
includes the Occidental Hotel, city hall, and the county court house properties.

Source: Modified after Digital Sanborn Maps
drafting by Bighorn Technical Design, Buffalo, Wyoming

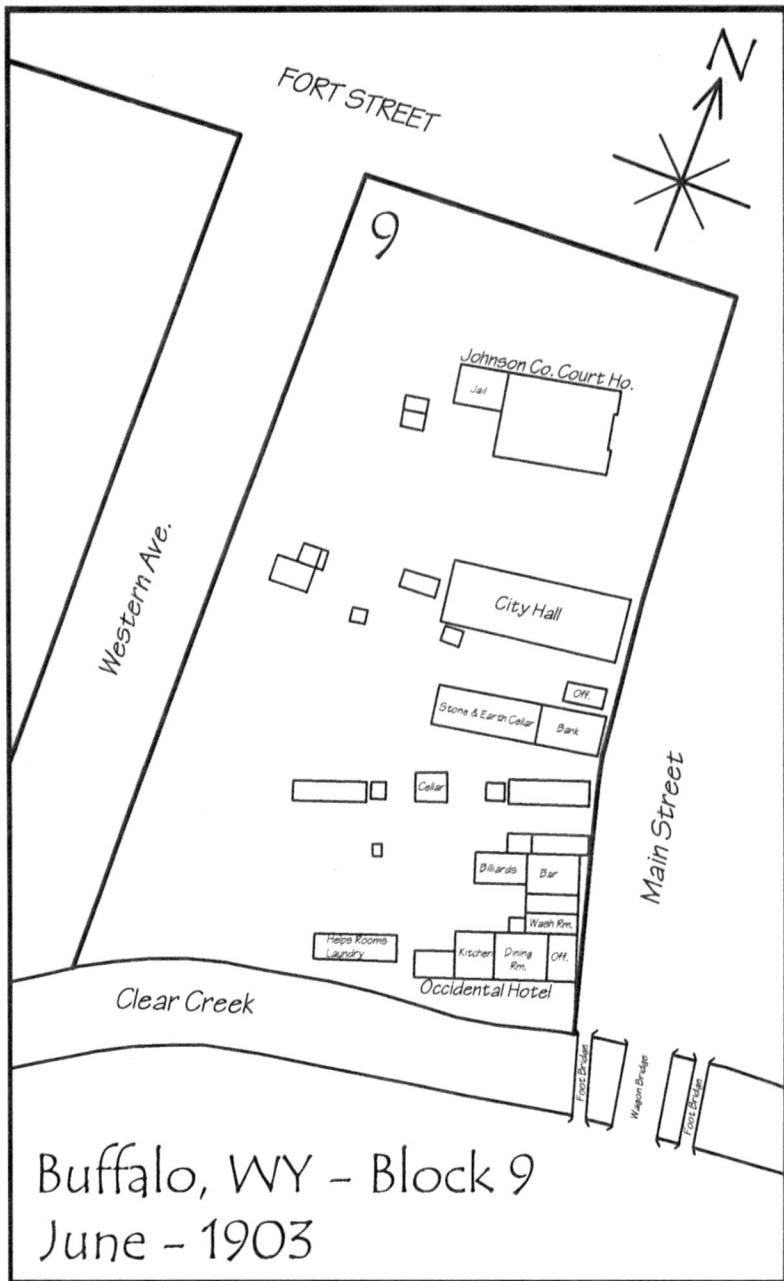

FORT STREET

9

Johnson Co. Court Ho.

Jail

Western Ave.

City Hall

Off.

Stone & Earth Cellar | Bank

Cellar

Main Street

Billiards | Bar

Wash Rm.

Helps Rooms Laundry

Kitchen | Dining Rm. | Off.

Occidental Hotel

Clear Creek

Foot Bridge

Wagon Bridge

Foot Bridge

Buffalo, WY – Block 9
June – 1903

Buffalo Street Plan – 1903
This map shows the west side of the first block of Main Street North that
includes the Occidental Hotel, city hall, and the county courthouse properties.

Source: Modified after Digital Sanborn Maps
drafting by Bighorn Technical Design, Buffalo, Wyoming

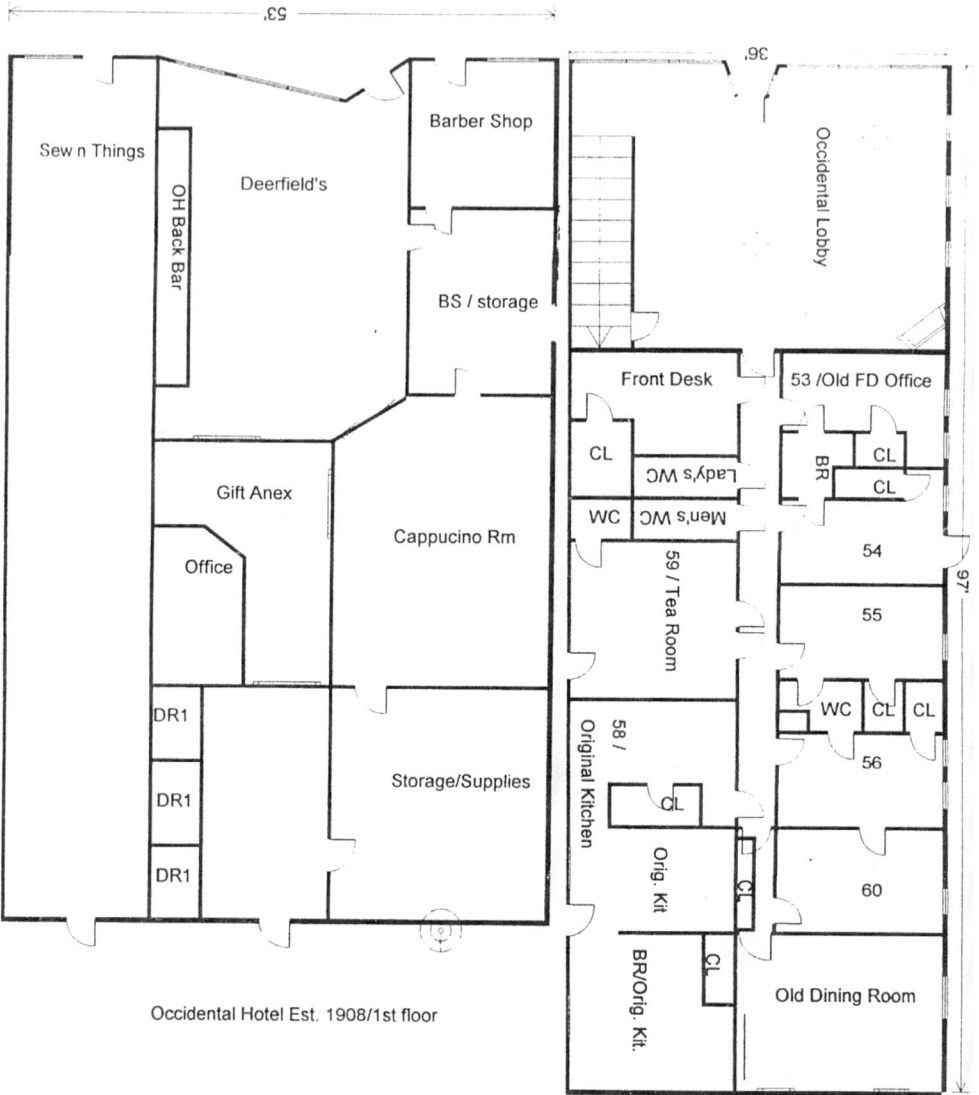

Occidental Hotel Est. 1908/1st floor

Occidental Hotel Est. 1910

Occidental First Floor Plan

This first floor plan shows the sections that were built in 1908 and 1910.
The date of the use or business in each room is judged to be in the mid-to
late-1990s. North is to the left.

Source: Author's collection

Occidental Hotel Est. 1903/2nd floor   Occidental Hotel Est. 1908/2nd floor

Occidental Hotel Est. 1910/2nd floor

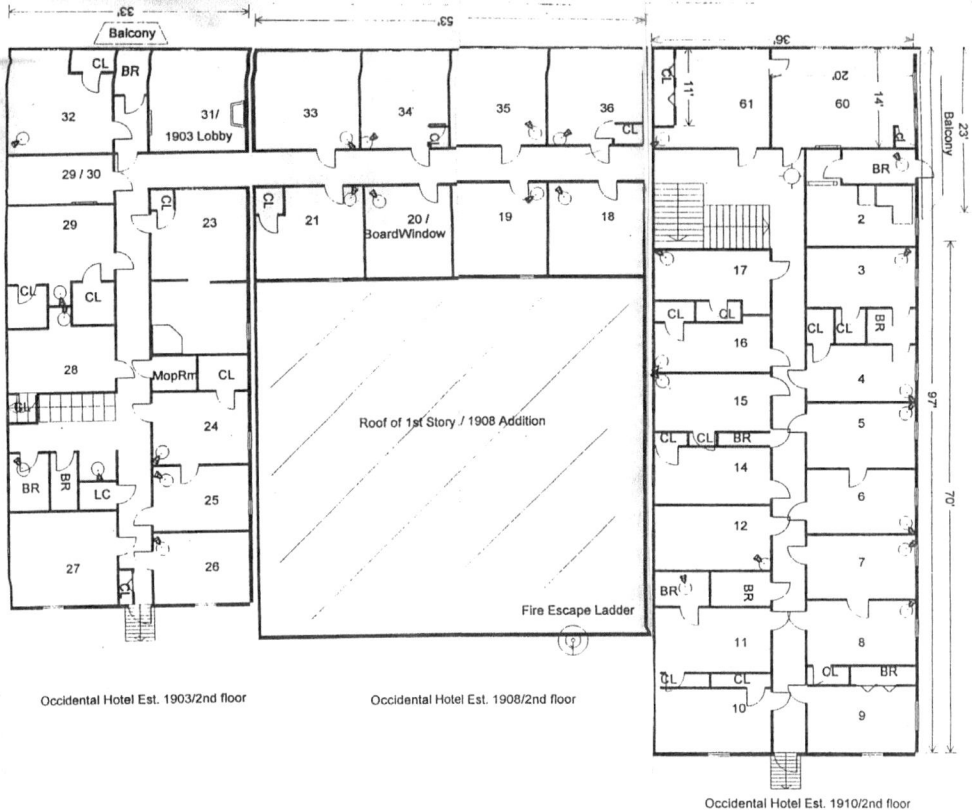

Occidental Second Floor Plan

This second floor plan shows the sections that were built in 1903, 1908, and 1910. The date of the use for each room is judged to be in the mid-to late-1990s. North is to the left.

Source: Author's collection

Occidental Advertisement

This advertisement appeared in the *Buffalo Bulletin* of December 22, 1910. Why the hotel is referred to as the "Annex" is unclear as the entire new brick structure is complete as the right-hand portion of the advertisement indicates. Also, Warren & Company are proprietors while Quick and Waegele are the owners.

Source: Author's collection

Occidental Hotel Annex

WARREN & CO.
Proprietors

Buffalo, - Wyo.

First class in every respect, steam heat, running hot and cold water, rooms with bath, up-to-date buffet, barber shop, spacious and convenient sample room. Beautiful scenery from veranda of hotel. Four miles from foot of Big Horn mountains.

Unexcelled trout stream within a few feet of the hotel. Miles of mountain trout fishing —finest in the world.

Fine camping grounds at convenient distances.

Rates:

Transient, $2.50 per day.

Special rates by the day or month.

The 1912 Flood
Two views of the damage to the Occidental Hotel and Clear Creek Bridge
following the flood.   Source: Occidental Hotel and Museum collection

The new hotel was scarcely two years old when it was subjected
to an onslaught by nature. On June 11, 1912, a cloudburst occurred
over the Clear Creek drainage between the Big Horns and the
Soldiers and Sailors Home on the previous Fort McKinney property.
The resulting flood swept downstream causing considerable damage in Buffalo and taking one resident's life. Located on the creek's
bank, the Occidental incurred about $20,000 in damages of the

community's estimated total of $500,000. The Occidental's damages were due in part because its laundry building was swept against the new cement Clear Creek bridge and, acting as a temporary dam, caused debris and water to sweep through the lower parts of the hotel.[28] Repairs were made and the hotel was back in business.

The year 1916 was a particularly sad one in the history of the Occidental hotel. Founder, Charles E. Buell, and his wife, Jennie Herrick Buell, were both killed in one of the earliest automobile accidents in Johnson County on January 24.[29]

The 1912 Flood
Damage to the Occidental Hotel and Clear Creek Bridge following the flood.
Source: Wyoming State Archives

Cleanup after the 1912 Flood
The debris in the central portion of this photograph appears to be flood related.

Source: Wyoming State Archives

The Smith Family Era – 1917-1997

Eight Decades of Ownership

Brothers, Tom and Harry Smith, leased the Occidental from Beer between 1895 and 1899. In 1917, a second set of Smith brothers, Alfred M. and George E., no relation to the former pair, took over the hotel's management as owners. As recorded in the Johnson County Abstract of Titles, they purchased the Occidental Hotel on April 2, 1917 from O. N. Quick and Fred Waegele, paying each of them $25,000.

A short article in the *Buffalo Voice* of April 13, 1917, noted that the Occidental Hotel had been recently purchased by the Smith brothers and that Robert Pennewell (Pennywell) arrived from Cheyenne to take charge of the hotel's operations. A search of the *Buffalo Bulletin* for the same time period revealed no other entries concerning the sale. The absence of publicity concerning the transfer of ownership for Buffalo's premier business is puzzling. It is, however, compatible with the Smith family lore that Alfred and his brother George acquired ownership of the Occidental through a poker game. Of course, the acquisition may have been a simple purchase – we may never know for certain. However, other large capital investments by the Smiths in the $50,000 range for Buffalo businesses and not for land or cattle are not known. Assuming a high-stakes poker game was involved, what the winning hand was would be interesting to know.

Alfred and George were sons of pioneer rancher John R. Smith and wife, Agnes Delaney Smith. Ranchers themselves, the two men apparently had little direct interest in operating a large hotel. Hiring a suitable manager would prove to be a difficult task for them. The former owners, Quick and Waegele, were available to help initially but, as previously noted in the *Buffalo Voice* article, Pennewell, from the Chicago area, was hired as a hotel manager. It seems that Pennewell had grand plans for the Occidental that included new crystal, china, silver, and linens embossed or engraved with the words "Occidental Hotel" or letters "OH" on them, elegant new furnishings purchased in Omaha, Nebraska, etc. When Al Smith

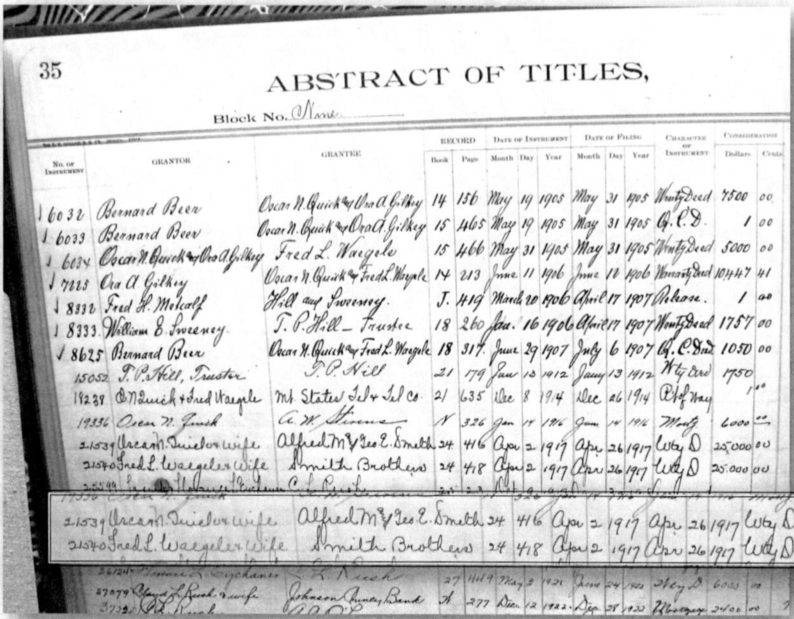

35

ABSTRACT OF TITLES,

Block No. Nine

No. of Instrument	Grantor	Grantee	Record Book	Record Page	Date of Instrument Month	Day	Year	Date of Filing Month	Day	Year	Character of Instrument	Consideration Dollars	Cents
6032	Bernard Beer	Oscar N. Quick & Ora A. Gilkey	14	156	May	19	1905	May	31	1905	Wnty Deed	7500	00
6033	Bernard Beer	Oscar N. Quick & Ora A. Gilkey	15	465	May	19	1905	May	31	1905	Q. C. D.	1	00
6034	Oscar N. Quick & Ora A. Gilkey	Fred L. Waegele	15	466	May	31	1905	May	31	1905	Wnty Deed	5000	00
7225	Ora A. Gilkey	Oscar N. Quick & Fred L. Waegele	14	213	June	11	1906	June	12	1906	Warranty Deed	10447	41
8332	Fred H. Metcalf	Hill and Sweeney	J.	419	March	20	1906	April	17	1907	Release	1	00
8333	William E. Sweeney	T. P. Hill – Trustee	18	260	Jan.	16	1906	April	17	1907	Wnty Deed	1757	00
8625	Bernard Beer	Oscar N. Quick & Fred L. Waegele	18	317	June	29	1907	July	6	1907	Q. C. Deed	1050	00
15052	T. P. Hill, Trustee	T. P. Hill	21	179	Jan	13	1912	Jany	13	1912	Wty Deed	1750	
19238	O. N. Quick & Fred Waegele	Mt. States Tel & Tel Co.	21	635	Dec	8	1914	Dec	26	1914	Rt of Way	1	00
19336	Oscar N. Quick	A. W. Stevens	N	326	Jan	14	1916	Jan	14	1916	Mortg	6000	00
21539	Oscar N. Quick & wife	Alfred M. & Geo. E. Smith	24	416	Apr	2	1917	Apr	26	1917	Wty D	25,000	00
21540	Fred L. Waegele & Wife	Smith Brothers	24	418	Apr	2	1917	Apr	26	1917	Wty D	25,000	00
26124	[illegible]	L. Rusk	27	419	May	3	1921	June	24	1921	Wty D	6000	00
27079	Claude L. Rusk & wife	Johnson County Bank	N	277	Dec.	12	1922	Dec	28	1922	Mortgage	2400	00

21539 Oscar N. Quick & wife Alfred M. & Geo. E. Smith 24 416 Apr 2 1917 Apr 26 1917 Wty D 25,000 00
21540 Fred L. Waegele & Wife Smith Brothers 24 418 Apr 2 1917 Apr 26 1917 Wty D 25,000 00

Johnson County Abstract of Titles

An Abstract of Title is a condensed history of the titles to a particular parcel of real estate, i.e., land, including buildings or improvements on it and its natural assets, e.g., minerals, water, etc. Above is page 35, Block No. 9, which lists the Occidental Hotel real estate owners from 1905 to 1922. The Smith Brothers purchase in 1917 is shown just below halfway on the listing and in the insert above it.

Source: Author's collection

Warranty Deed for the Occidental Hotel

Shown below is the Warranty Deed for the sale of the Occidental Hotel from Quick and his wife to the Smith brothers. It is on page 16 in the Johnson County records; page 18 lists a similar sale from Waegele and his wife to the brothers for the other one-half interest. A Warranty Deed is a deed where the grantor (seller) guarantees that he/she holds clear title to the piece of real estate and has the right to sell it to the grantee (buyer)

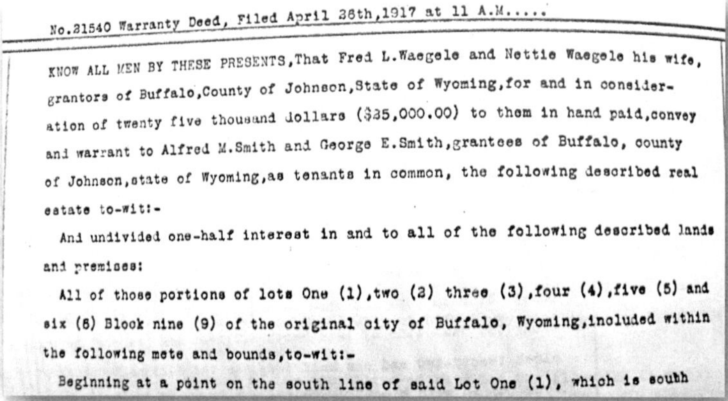

No.21540 Warranty Deed, Filed April 26th,1917 at 11 A.M.....

KNOW ALL MEN BY THESE PRESENTS,That Fred L.Waegele and Nettie Waegele his wife, grantors of Buffalo,County of Johnson,State of Wyoming,for and in consideration of twenty five thousand dollars ($25,000.00) to them in hand paid,convey and warrant to Alfred M.Smith and George E.Smith,grantees of Buffalo, county of Johnson,state of Wyoming,as tenants in common, the following described real estate to-wit:-

And undivided one-half interest in and to all of the following described lands and premises:

All of those portions of lots One (1),two (2) three (3),four (4),five (5) and six (6) Block nine (9) of the original city of Buffalo, Wyoming,included within the following mete and bounds,to-wit:-

Beginning at a point on the south line of said Lot One (1), which is south

Source: Author's collection

started receiving the bills for these exorbitant upgrades, Pennewell received his discharge.

After Pennewell, the management of the Occidental was very different. The roundup crew from the Smith Brothers ranch, located about 25 miles south of town, was brought to the hotel. The camp cook prepared the meals for the dining room while several cowboys ran the front desk and tavern and hired what help was needed for room cleaning, waiting on tables, and general operations. This was a functional, but not entirely satisfactory, long-term solution to the Occidental's management. There followed a succession of multiple managers, day clerks, and night clerks. Then, the September 4, 1919, *Buffalo Bulletin* reported that the Big Horn Resorts Company had leased the hotel for a "term of years"; they also owned the South Fork Inn at that time and planned to operate both facilities. How long this lease lasted is not known, but it was a "solution" to the Occidental's management tasks.

In 1921 or 1923, Alfred Smith appealed to his wife, Margaret Lothian Smith, whom he had married in 1907, to take over the management "for a few months until he could hire a new manager."

Alfred M. Smith and Margaret Lothian Smith – circa 1910s
Alfred and his brother George E. Smith acquired the Occidental Hotel and property in April of 1917. Margaret managed the hotel from 1921 to 1976.
Source: Smith family collection (A. M. Smith) and Occidental Hotel Museum collection (M. L. Smith)

Margaret with her sons,
Alfred L. and Robert C.
Alfred (left) and "Robbie"
(right) of Margaret; c. 1914
Source: Smith family collection

She agreed and then, after trying to manage the hotel from a house in Buffalo, Margaret Smith moved herself and two sons, Alfred L. and Robert C., into the Occidental. She ended up running the hotel for more than 50 years until 1976 when she died at age 94. Margaret's longevity as Occidental manager made her synonymous with the "the Occidental" to generations of residents and hotel guests.

Margaret was born in Scotland in 1881 and came to Buffalo with her parents in 1884. At 16 years old, she was a member of the second graduating class of Buffalo's new high school. She then taught as a normal teacher (an elementary school teacher without a degree) in local schools at Greub, Willow Grove, and Meeteetse for several years. In 1900, Margaret enrolled at the University of Wyoming and graduated in 1903 with a degree in pedagogy (teaching) – one of Johnson County's early graduates from the university. She was also a member of the university's first female ROTC class. A year prior to her graduation at age 21, Margaret was elected Johnson County Superintendent of Schools, the youngest person ever to hold that position. She was re-elected the year she took over the management of the Occidental.

Margaret was well qualified to manage the multi-task operations of a large hotel even though she had no formal business or management training. At the time, Margaret was already keeping the financial accounting records for three family ranch companies. The managerial and personnel experience as school superintendent, coupled with the extensive ranch accounting, served her well in the new job of hotel manager. Obviously very well, as a temporary position expanded to more than half-century duration.

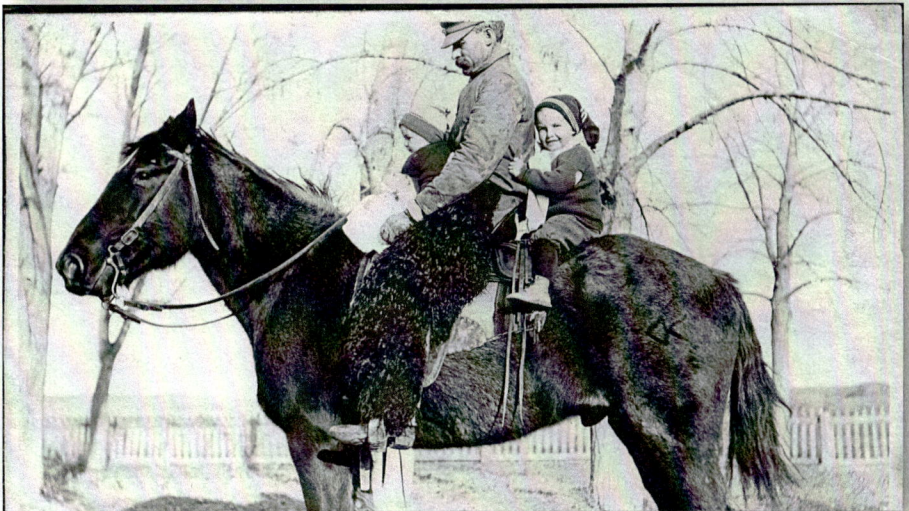

Alfred M. Smith and sons – Undated

Source: Smith family collection

Margaret Lothian – Late 1880s
Margaret at eighth grade commencement (upper left: 1893; back row – second
from right) and at high school graduation (right; 1897).

Source: Smith family collection

The following incident during the 1930s Depression is an example
of her staff hiring process. Carl Aegerter was drifting across the country trying to find some type of employment. He came to Buffalo with
his young wife but while here the welfare worker, Ruth Martin, urged
them to continue on as there were no local funds available for help.
It is thought that Martin put the young couple up for the night in
the Occidental. Smith learned that Aegerter was looking for a job
and asked him, "What can you do?" His response was that he could
learn to do most anything. Satisfied, Smith took the man to the New
York Store on Main Street, a dry goods store, advanced him money
for some new clothes (a grand sum of $2.50) and then made him
the Occidental's new night clerk. Aegerter repaid this helpful start by
eventually becoming a successful Buffalo businessman. He owned a
number of businesses, including a motel on Fort Street.

Margaret Lothian – University of
Wyoming Graduation – 1903
Source: Smith family collection

Margaret Lothian –
Teacher and Administrator
Margaret's teacher's certificate
(upper) and her letterhead
stationery as County
Superintendent of Schools.
Source: Smith family collection

COUNTY SUPERINTENDENT OF SCHOOLS
JOHNSON COUNTY, WYOMING
MARGARET LOTHIAN SMITH

BUFFALO, WYOMING

Margaret Lothian and Oscar Bowman – Wedding Picture
On March 11, 1957, Margaret married her childhood sweetheart, J. Oscar
Bowman. A resident of Buffalo for more than 50 years, Bowman had moved to
California where he worked in business management positions.

Source: Smith family collection

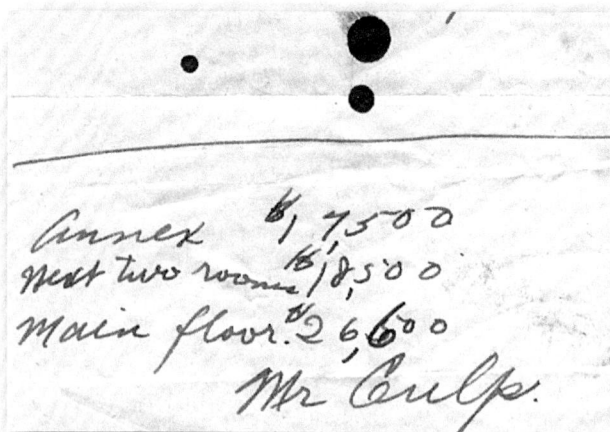

Poker Game Marker for the Occidental Hotel?
A marker is an I.O.U. or credit voucher granted to a poker player by "the
house" or by the other players in the game. Without any explanation the piece
of paper above was found among the early Occidental files. It is speculated that
it may have been a poker game marker for the Occidental that lists a total value
of $62,600. Culp was the contractor that built the brick Occidental buildings;
he may have provided the value estimates for the marker.

Source: Occidental Hotel and Museum collection

STEAM HEAT   HOT AND COLD WATER IN EVERY ROOM   EUROPEAN PLAN

OCCIDENTAL HOTEL
SMITH BROS., Proprietors

Money paid out by Smith Bros
for Occidental Hotel

BUFFALO, WYOMING,   191

To Stock Growers	Cv.	6000.00	
" "	Cv.	1017.00	
" Adams & Young	Cv.	2809.09	
" P & Sheehan	Cv.	900.00	
" A. N. Stevens	Cv.	108.00	
"	Cv.	4000.00	
" J N Stevenson	Cv.	4.50	
" Occidental Hotel	Cv.	1236.69	
" "	Cv.	5165.57	
" Stock Growers	Cv.	1700.00	
" "	Cv.	89.12	
" "	Cv.	1.50	
" Occidental Hotel	Cv.	2700.00	
" "		600.00	?
" Chg on Rug	Cv.	27.50	
" Beef	Cv.	291.77	
" Occidental	Cv.	2000.00	?
		28650.00	

Less cash 1500 00   2093.90
Acct   593.90 #26556.10
             2093.90

Occidental Hotel Voucher – circa 1910s

This cost listing was found in the Occidental files. Its relationship, if any, to the suspected "marker" is not known. Note, however, that the $26,556 total here is similar to the $26,000 value for the "Main Floor" on the marker. The Smith brothers' ownership began on April 2, 1917.

Source: Occidental Hotel and Museum collection

Another night clerk was Joseph Avander, hired in the late 1940s. He was a sheepherder at the time, but his health would not let him continue. Smith learned of his situation and gave him an inside job. He worked at that position until he died in 1957.

Margaret Smith's "trademark" characteristic was her deep commitment to the value of education. As she encountered promising rural students in her role as Superintendent, she saw them through high school by giving them room and board at the Occidental in exchange for helping at the hotel. A specific example of this process was long-time resident, Fanny Sackett, who babysat for Smith in exchange for staying at the hotel while attending the Johnson County High School. A much less well-known aspect of this educating of youngsters was the fact that over the years a sizeable number of them were Native Americans. There was still some prejudice against them among the general public but none with Smith.

Riding Party in Front of the Occidental
Both the purpose and date of this group of riders and carriage on Main Street
are not known; a picnic outing on Clear Creek towards the Big Horns for out
of state visitors? Main Street is not paved and no automobiles are shown.
Source: Occidental Hotel and Museum collection

The above examples are illustrative of the use of business to help
fellow citizens in a manner where both parties benefited. Margaret
Smith's longevity as Occidental manager linked that positive, generous
public attitude with the hotel's long-standing reputation for hospitality.

Three financial documents in the Smith family's files that deal
with hotel operations during the Margaret Smith era were located.
There is a 1935 Department of Commerce Census of Business report
for the hotel and two Occidental Tavern reports; a 1949 Partnership
Agreement for its operation and a First Quarter 1952 Profit and
Loss Statement. The total amount of information in those papers
is skimpy but does provide a bit of insight into the Occidental's fi-
nances during the mid-20th century.

The Census of Business report lists the hotel's total operating
receipts for 1935 at $13,500 – Room Rental $9,500 and House
Rental $4,000. A Net Profit number is not given but the Percentage
Occupancy is stated as 60%. The partnership document is between
Margaret Smith and Marvin Jones for purchase of the tavern's business
license and equipment from Vincent Klinkhammer for $20,000. Each
party would pay half that amount; Jones would then take a weekly

New Brick Occidental and the Clear Creek Bridge – circa mid-1900s
Above are views of the new Occidental building that was completed in 1910.
The Main Street bridge and the hotel's proximity to Clear Creek are seen.
Judging by the street light fixtures, the upper photograph is the earlier; note
also that the name Occidental does not appear above the windows.

Source: Occidental Hotel and Museum collection

salary of $70 and the hotel a monthly rental fee of $150. Those costs were added to the general expense of operation and any resulting net profit was divided between the two parties. For the year 1952 that net profit would be in the $1,200-$1,300 range according to the First Quarter Statement. The numbers for that quarter were: income $12,100 (bar sales $11,700 and vending machine receipts $300) and total expenses $11,700 (inventory $7,000 and expenses $4,700). The specific net profit number listed on the statement was $446. [30]

Margaret Smith had two successful marriages. After Alfred M. Smith died in 1934, she married a childhood sweetheart, J. Oscar Bowman in 1967.

After her death in 1976, the hotel was willed to her grandchildren and managed by Irene Voiles Smith, wife of Alfred L. Smith. During the latter half of the 1970s under Irene's management, the hotel did a brisk business as coal miners from the Gillette coal boom scrambled for utility apartments and cheap rentals (Occidental room let for $25 per week). From 1976 to 1982, Irene, ("Occidental Lil" as her husband called her), repainted, re-carpeted, and refurbished every room in the hotel, doing much of the work herself. On one occasion, she told a plumber about water leaks in the crawl space which she called "The Black Hole of Calcutta" after crawling through it. She reserved one room which she called "The Drunk Tank" because the town jail found it cheaper to house those folks there than to have to clean each jail cell on a frequent basis; Irene refused to rent it to anyone else.

Once the Department of Labor did an inspection and Irene was asked if she was an "Equal Opportunity Employer." She replied, "Well, let's see. My day manager, Mr. Jolly, is a retired grocer; Walt, my night man is crippled and wears a leg brace; my housekeeping staff includes a deaf woman, a naturalized citizen from Mexico, and a college student. I think I qualify." Irene continued to manage the hotel and bus stop with storefront rentals until 1982 when she turned over operations to the grandchildren of Margaret Smith Bowman.

The Occidental Hotel operated for about a year longer until 1983 when it was closed to all but the few remaining long-term residents. Then, in January 1984, it closed completely. It was reopened in 1990 at the urging of Jeanette Burris McCain to be ready for an upcoming, commemorative program dealing with the 1892 Cattle War. Thirty-five volunteers helped with clean up in preparation for the reopening. In 1991, one hundred volunteers worked in the hotel for special events during the summer months and greeted visitors for self-guided tours.

Occidental Hotel Postcards – mid 1920s
Lobby of Occidental Hotel   Sources: Ken and Sue Heuermann collection

Occidental Lobby – 1927
The clerk in this photograph is Harley Fisher; the only other man
identified is George Weber in the white shirt and vest.
                              Source: Occidental Hotel and Museum collection

The biggest deterioration of the hotel itself was during the
"dead" period from closing in 1984 to reopening in 1990. Some
maintenance was thereafter possible and it continued in that mode
until purchased by John and Dawn Wexo in 1997.

Rental of Occidental Store Front Space by Small Businesses

Rentals of the Main Street storefront spaces in the Occidental were made from its earliest days. The Stockgrowers Bank of Buffalo was an early tenant of the new brick Occidental building in 1908. Over the ensuing years there were a number of different businesses occupying these spaces for varying lengths of time. Perhaps one of the most long-lived was the barbershop located next to the tavern. Additionally, there was a range of specialty shops, flower stores, clothing stores, business offices, e.g., the public gas company, etc. that took advantage of the excellent Main Street location. The Occidental also leased a separate building near Clear Creek that housed a small diner, the Busy Bee. In later years, it gained fame as the "Lazy Fly" of Sagebrush Sven's column in the *Buffalo Bulletin*.

All of these rentals brought income to the Occidental's coffers. That income became more essential as the guest business declined. The hotel was eventually closed, but the rentals continued and their business activity and rent proceeds kept theft, vandalism, and decay at a minimum. They were also a constant reminder to the community that their iconic structure needed help.

Alfred L. (1909-1995) and Irene Voiles Smith (1919-1985) Pictured at their 25th wedding anniversary in 1975. Irene operated and managed the Occidental Hotel from 1976 to 1982, directing upgrades and maintenance during that time.

Source: Smith family collection

Occidental Hotel Postcards – circa 1930s – 40s
Buffalo's Main Street looking south.
Upper: Postmarked 1933.
Lower: c. 1940s.
Note that Main Street is now paved and that there are parking meters.

Source: Ken and Sue Heuermann collection

Grant Stroter – the Occidental Shoeshiner

The shoeshiner or boot polisher is a person who polishes men's shoes with shoe polish for a small fee. They are also called shoeshine boys and bootblacks. It is not an esteemed occupation.

Stroter's Shoeshine Stand

This is the stand that Grant Stroter used for shining shoes outside the Occidental Hotel. Complete with its spittoon which was placed on the sidewalk next to the stand. It is now on display in the restored Occidental Tavern. (Note: A head mount of the rare Wyoming jackalope is behind the stand.)

Source: Author's collection

However, several well-known public figures worked as shoeshine boys, including Rush Limbaugh radio talk show host and Lee Trevino, professional golfer. With the use of synthetic materials in shoes, they are now seldom seen in this country.

For many years, Grant Stroter shined shoes in front of the Occidental Hotel. Just how long is not known but he lived in Buffalo for 40 years and worked at several business establishments before passing away on September 17, 1947. According to his obituary in the **Buffalo Bulletin** *(Sept. 18, 1947) Stroter was born on November 4, 1868 in St. Joseph, Missouri and married "Tommi" Whitbear in 1918 at Lusk, Wyoming. He was well liked in the community and Fred Gray told the author that businesses closed for two hours the day of his funeral. During his lifetime in Buffalo, he and his wife were the only African-American residents of that community.*

Stroter's Headstone
The grave marker in Buffalo's Willow Grove Cemetery for Grant and his wife, Tommi, is shown above.   Source: Author's collection

The Busy Bee

The Busy Bee café was started by Bill and Sarah Voiles. It served a short order menu by counter service only. Diners apparently began in the northeastern U.S. but with time, spread throughout the country. They were the precursors to today's fast food restaurants in that they served a wide range of short-order foods, fostered a casual atmosphere, and maintained late operating hours. On the other hand, they had more individuality than the fast food chains, even though there was a certain degree of similarity from one to the other.

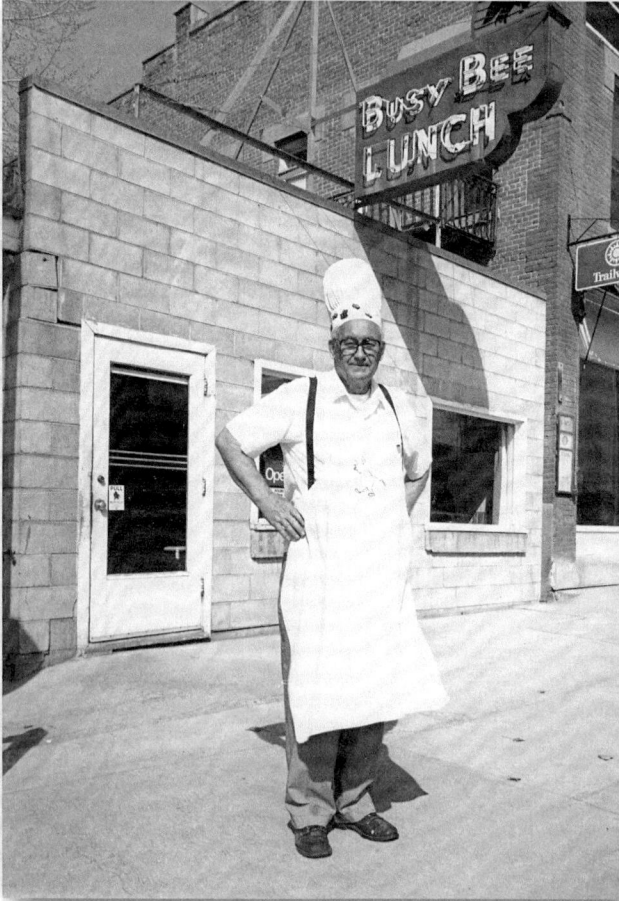

Hollis Voiles and the Busy Bee
Source: Voiles family collection

The Busy Bee became iconic under the management of Voiles' son Hollis and his wife Helen. From the 1940s until the 1980s, the Busy Bee and "Hollis" became synonymous. Helen was reputed to be the world's best pie maker and everyone had their favorites among her fruit and cream pies. The number of the pies that she baked was also legendary. She made 20 pies a day for 6 days a week for 40 years which totals a quarter-of-a-million pies! Her descendants figured it this way: each pie was nine-inches wide – laid end to end the total would reach from Buffalo to Casper – 2-1/2 times. In the bed of her pick-up truck she had a special wooden pie-hauler box made to transport the pies from her home, where she did all the baking, to the Busy Bee. They arrived there each morning at about ten a.m. One of her pie fans, Mike Sullivan of Casper, had a number of them flown to Cheyenne for his Inauguration Party when he was elected governor.

Hollis' food was every bit as popular as his wife's pies. Among his customers' favorite items were pancakes, omelets, eggs and ham steaks, burgers and fries, and chili. However, as good as the food was at the Busy Bee, it was really Hollis' personality and character that "made" the place such a success. He treated everyone the same, your financial or social status made no difference to him; local citizens enjoyed talking with him and meeting their friends at his counter. He knew what his regulars would order and, when he saw them coming, he had it waiting for them.

The Busy Bee's popularity grew to the stage that there were waiting lines for each of the 22 counter stools from about 11 a.m. to 1 p.m. and then from 6 p.m. to 8 p.m. Hollis is said to have had a saying that he used rather routinely: "We aren't busy until they are standing three deep waiting for a seat so don't complain until they're three deep."

Local ranchers were among the regular Busy Bee customers. In particular, elderly Eli Espinosa who brought his shearing crew to shear at the ranches of the Basque and other sheepmen each year. During that time he brought his crew to the Busy Bee for some of their meals. When he did, he would give Hollis a container of his secret hot sauce for the shearers to use as it was a favorite of theirs. One fall, Espinosa told Hollis that he was going to die and would give him the recipe for use with the shearers in the future. Hollis made light of the comment but he accepted the recipe. Later that year, the elderly man passed away.

A Busy Bee claim-to-fame was its involvement in the making of two motion picture films – one indirectly and one directly. The indirect association was with a 1963 Robert Taylor film entitled <u>Miracle of the White Stallions</u>. Taylor played an Austrian colonel in WWII who protected his beloved Lipizzaner stallions to make certain they were surrendered into the right hands for proper treatment. While in Austria filming, Taylor, a Busy Bee regular when staying at his ranch north of Buffalo, had four cases of Hollis' chili in canning jars flown there for use at a party Taylor was giving for the film crew. The direct Busy Bee filming was in Endangered Species starring Robert Urich in 1982. He played a vacationing ex-cop out west who helps a small town sheriff investigate a strange case of cattle mutilations. Several scenes were filmed in the Busy Bee; the crew spent a total of two days there. Both Hollis and Helen appeared in the picture.

The preceding is just a sampling of the many Busy Bee stories that the Voiles descendants have to tell. Daughter Christy Voiles Washut shared them with the author in a delightful interview. The family business was sold to Dottie Jenkins in the mid-1980s.

A final note illustrates the high regard that Occidental manager Margaret Smith held for the Voiles family – a 100-year lease to the Busy Bee property to protect them and their business during her lifetime and after she passed away.

Chronology of Occidental Ownership

The following dates were derived from the Johnson County Abstract of Titles. Dates with the year only were taken from the published literature.

1879-1881	Buell
1881-1888	Buell, McCray
1888-1891	McCray
1891, June 29-1892, Sept. 23	Hathaway
1892, Sept. 23-Mar. 26, 1903	Beer
Mar. 26, 1903-May 19, 1905	Quick, Gilkey
May 31, 1905-Apr. 2, 1917	Quick, Gilkey, Waegele
Apr. 2, 1917-1997	Smith (brothers)
1997-Present	Wexo

The Wexo Restoration – 1997 to Present

In 1997, John and Dawn Wexo purchased the Occidental Hotel. Relocating from California, they required a new home for their Knowledge Company's publication business. That company featured the *Zoobooks*, a series of colorful and informative children's books created and authored by John. First published in 1983, the series became very successful – acquiring hundreds of thousand of subscribers, winning the 2001 Parent Choice Gold Award, and made available worldwide in nine languages.

The Wexos were fascinated with the historic Occidental Hotel and much of its original furnishings, objects, and wide ranges of memorabilia were still present. Collectively, they provided a unmistakable frontier ambience. Everything was in disarray, making clean up and restoration a daunting task. It was the Wexos' intent from the onset to honor the fine old structure by restoration whereever possible and replication elsewhere.

They determined to make the first floor into a hotel museum open to the public. They moved their Knowledge Company's corporate headquarters into the second floor and set to work restoring the first floor to its "first layer" condition. They applied for federal non-profit tax status 501 (c)(3) and joined the American Association of Museums in Washington, D.C., as initial administrative steps in establishing an Occidental Hotel Museum.

The Wexos were in Buffalo only a few years when, in the early 2000s, world events – the 9/11 attack, the Iraq War, petroleum prices, etc. – caused severe impacts on the U.S. economy. The cumulative result for the Wexos was that they were forced to abandon their publication efforts. At that stage, they decided not only to restore the Occidental as a hotel museum but to develop it into an operational hotel. Their task was certainly cut out for them.

The Occidental Hotel had been well built and was still structurally sound, with some 27,000 square feet of space in 60 rooms. It was, however, in a state of neglect, resulting in serious deterioration of floors, ceilings, stairways, tiles, walls, plumbing, and electrical circuits. The rooms were still filled with antique furniture, some dating to the early 1880s, which were in generally good condition. They alone were a treasure trove of early Western history. The Wexos were won over by the Occidental's historic role as the heartbeat of the community. Re-establishing it as a hotel would restore that century-plus service.

The physical restoration involved the removal of several layers of paint from walls, woodwork, and ceilings followed by repainting; replacing floor rugs, plumbing, and electrical fixtures – all in period correct materials and designs. For such a large structure, this was an enormous undertaking that would take several years of dedicated effort and more than $1 million in expense. The lobby and back area were restored first; restoration of the bar alone took a year and a half. Additionally, everything had to be brought to present-day civic codes *and* in conformity with the building's National Register of Historic Places listing.

The following description of the restoration process is from John Wexo's website:

> She [Dawn] suspected that there was a "historic gem" under all of the dilapidation. As it turned out, she was right. Gradually, as multiple layers of ancient and unyielding paint were scraped away, and multiple thicknesses of decaying carpet were pulled up, the grand old Occidental began to reveal itself. And it was even more intact and splendid than Dawn had suspected.

> On the first floor, all of the wonderful decorated tin ceiling proved to be in perfect condition. The wooden floors under the dead carpets were in fine shape (with the exception of the dance floor in the saloon, which needed to be jacked up five inches on one side).

> During the 1940s and 1950s, false ceilings and walls had been installed to "modernize" the saloon. When these were pulled down, beautiful original wainscoting and intricately embossed wall covering were brought out of hiding. The cellars and attics of the Occidental proved to be bulging with historic furnishings and architectural details that could be re-conditioned and re-installed.

Before and After Restoration
The Occidental Hotel as it appeared in the early 1900s (upper) and in the early 2000s. Only minor changes, awnings and signage, have been made to the exterior.

Sources: Upper – Jim Dillinger collection
Lower – Occidental Hotel Museum collection

Restoration in progress on the Ceilings, Floors, and Heating Systems
Source: Occidental Hotel and Museum collection

Restoration in progress on the Stairways and Balconies
Source: Occidental Hotel and Museum collection

Additionally, John attributed this serendipity of condition and collected antiques to long-term manager, Margaret Smith Bowman:

> This was partly because Margaret Smith was naturally frugal, but it was also because the Occidental Hotel became the focus and joy of her life.

> Instead of ripping out ornate tin ceilings, she covered them up with false ceilings and walls, or simply a coat of paint. When the need to "modernize" the hotel led to the purchase of new furnishings, the old ones were often stored away instead of junked.

> In this way, the Occidental Hotel became a kind of time capsule, just waiting for somebody to come along and "dig it up." And two women who never knew each other – Margaret Smith and Dawn Wexo – worked together (in a manner of speaking) to bring about the survival of the unique historic treasure that is the Occidental Hotel.

An early recognition of the Wexos' work was the 1999 Wyoming State Historical Society Maurine Carley Award for Historic Preservation. Later awards were the 2007 and 2008 "Best Hotel in the West" awards by *True West* magazine.

Buffalo and county residents were delighted that their iconic structure was restored to operation. As a community they returned, or helped recover, many items that had been in the old hotel – a billiard table, the bar's stained glass doors, a piano, doilies, rugs, even an Occidental token from the turn of the century. On of the more unusual items were Margaret Smith's 100-year-old plants, which were returned in 1997, the first year of restoration. The broad, spiny-leaf African begonias were a favorite of Margaret's and had been cared for by a friend for decades.

Contributions from locals continue. In February 2007, Mike Stanley provided his collection of restored antique radios, plus a low power AM transmitter, to play music from the 1920s to the 1940s throughout the hotel. These radios are located throughout the hotel.

With time, dedication, hard work, and capital investment, the Wexos brought the Occidental Hotel to full museum and operational hotel status. A $150,000 Community Development Grant to which they provided $48,000 in matching funds provided early assistance. It was not easy and there were indeed "bumps" along the way, but they remained true to their commitment to honor the old "Lady." In so doing, they now make the experience of a historical hotel routinely available to the public.[31]

Occidental Memorabilia

As an historic hotel and museum, virtually everything in the Occidental is an antique or artifact dating from the late 1880s to the mid-1900s. Items of a wide range are dispersed throughout the hotel in a structured but informal manner rather than the formal, interpretive exhibits typical of today's museum settings. This presentation complements nicely the setting provided by the antique furnishings in general and routine use in all of the hotel spaces. While in the Occidental, the visitor is immersed in a frontier-era hotel environment that is delightful to experience.

There is one exhibit case containing a number of small items found during the building restoration in drawers, shelves, and boxes. Several items are depicted in the following illustrations.

Restoration –
Recognition of a job well done.
Source:
Occidental Hotel and Museum collection

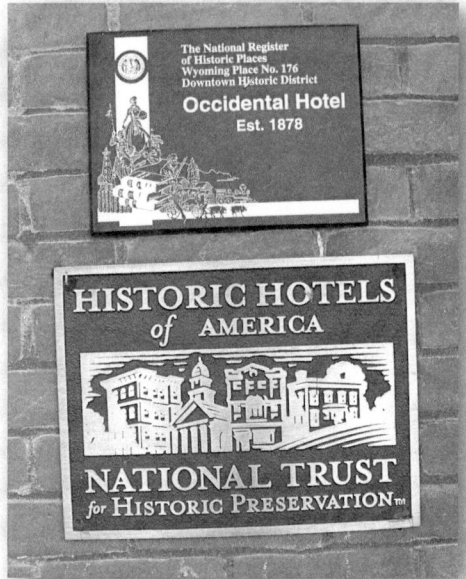

MUSEUM OF THE OCCIDENTAL HOTEL

AN HISTORIC FRONTIER HOTEL

WELCOME TO THE OPENING CELEBRATION OF THE MUSEUM OF THE OCCIDENTAL HOTEL

DEC. 5TH-6TH, 1997

HOSTED BY THE WILD BUNCH!

WELCOME!

WE WELCOME YOU TO THE COMPLETION OF THE FIRST STAGE IN THE RESTORATION OF THE OCCIDENTAL HOTEL. THE RE-OPENING OF THE HISTORIC OCCIDENTAL IS A TIME OF GREAT ANTICIPATION AND CELEBRATION. CHILDREN'S BOOKS OF AMERICA AND ZOOBOOKS ARE PROUD TO HAVE DONATED THE FUNDS TO MAKE THIS FIRST STAGE A REALITY. WE HOPE TO BRING BACK THE BEAUTY AND SPLENDOR OF THIS HISTORIC FRONTIER HOTEL WITH THE CONTINUED SUPPORT OF THE MANY FRIENDS OF THE OCCIDENTAL AND THE BUFFALO COMMUNITY.

MUSEUM OF THE OCCIDENTAL HOTEL REOPENS!

THE OCCIDENTAL HOTEL IS NOW A REGISTERED NON-PROFIT MUSEUM. WE PLAN TO HAVE THE MUSEUM OPEN TO VISITORS DURING THE SUMMER TOURIST SEASON. DURING THE WINTER MONTHS THE OCCIDENTAL WILL SERVE ITS TRADITIONAL FUNCTION AS A GATHERING PLACE FOR THE BUFFALO COMMUNITY. OVER THE NEXT 3 YEARS, WITH YOUR HELP, WE PLAN TO BRING THE OCCIDENTAL BACK TO ITS TURN-OF-THE CENTURY GLORY IN 5 STAGES.

* *STAGE 1:* REOPENING OF THE LOBBY, TEA ROOM, PARLOR AND DOWNSTAIR'S GUEST ROOMS.
* *STAGE 2:* WINTER OF '98, RESTORE THE OCCIDENTAL SALOON AND BILLIARD'S PARLOR.
* *STAGE 3:* SPRING OF '98, BEGIN CURATORIAL WORK ON THE PHOTO-GRAPHS, HISTORICAL OBJECTS AND JOURNALS IN PREPARATION FOR DISPLAY IN THREE MAIN GALLERIES THROUGHOUT THE MUSEUM.

A NON-PROFIT MUSEUM & COMMUNITY MEETING PLACE!

* *STAGE 4:* SUMMER OF '98 - SPRING OF 99, RESTORATION OF THE EXTERIOR OF THE OCCIDENTAL.
* *STAGE 5:* SUMMER OF '99, MARKS THE RECREATION OF THE VICTORIAN TEA GARDEN ALONG THE BANKS OF CLEAR CREEK.

IN ORDER FOR THE RESTORATION AND PLANNED JUNE 1998 PUBLIC REOPENING OF THE OCCIDENTAL TO BECOME A REALITY, WE WILL NEED YOUR HELP. ANY DONATION - WHETHER FINANCIAL OR THE LOAN OF AN OBJECT RELATED TO THE OCCIDENTAL HOTEL - WILL BE GREATLY APPRECIATED.

Many Thanks for Your Support!

John, Dawn and Zoe

THE OCCIDENTAL HOTEL IS NOW A REGISTERED NON-PROFIT MUSEUM APPLYING FOR 501-3-C FEDERAL TAX EXEMPT STATUS

CONTACT FIRST INTERSTATE BANK OF BUFFALO FOR TIMED DONATIONS

FOR GIFTS OR LOANS OF OBJECTS, CALL: (307) 684-0451

Brochure – Hotel Museum Opening – Dec. 5-6, 1997
Source: Occidental Hotel and Museum collection

Occidental Hotel Lobby – Museum Entrance
This recent photo of the Occidental lobby conveys the warmth and frontier
ambience of the antique furnishings and period decorations that greet the
museum visitor. The doorway on the right looks into a hallway of historic
photos and artifacts related to the hotel's origin and early years.

Source: Occidental Hotel and Museum collection

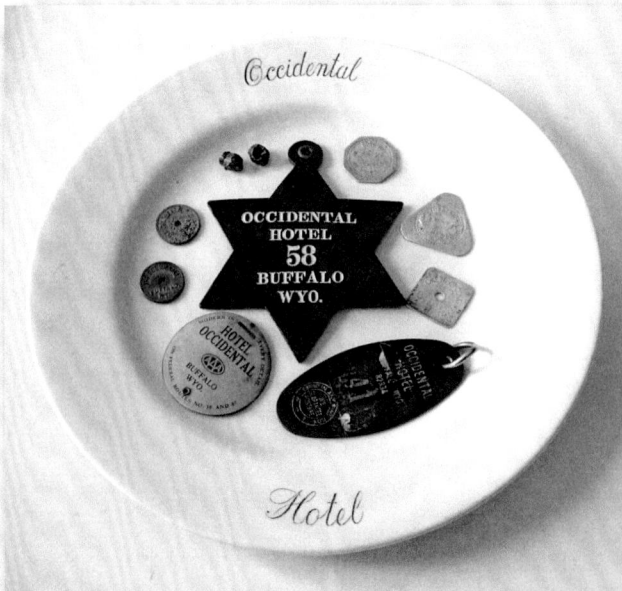

Hotel Items
An early Occidental
Hotel plate with
room key holders,
Occidental tokens,
and at the 11
o'clock position,
two .38 caliber lead
bullets removed
from the bar room
walls.
Source: Occidental
Hotel and Museum
collection

Occidental Tokens

Close-ups of two tokens in the preceding photograph. Left: "Occidental Bar Buffalo, Wyo." and "Good for 1 Drink" with two letters, S W (?) stamped on the token. Right: "The Occidental Buffalo, Wyo." and "Good for 12-1/2 cents in Trade." Source: Occidental Hotel and Museum collection

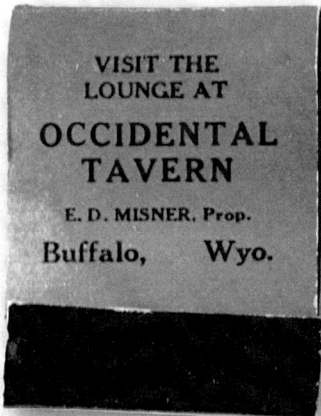

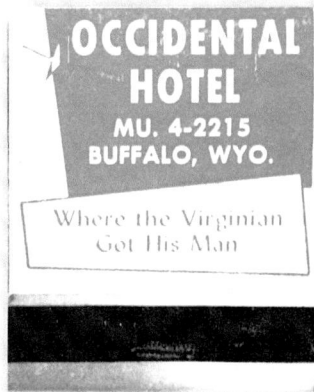

Occidental Book Matches – Dates unknown
Source: Occidental Hotel and Museum collection

Occidental Bar Whiskey Flask
An early Red Top Rye whiskey flask
from the Occidental Bar.

Source: Occidental Hotel and Museum
collection

Occidental Charge Keys
These charge keys were used to
record hotel guests' (by room
number) purchases by punching
paper forms rather than writing on
them – faster and more accurate.
The items listed are, from the
top down: Special, Drayage,
Bath, Laundry, Telegram, Phone,
Pressing, Café, and Cigars.

Source: Occidental Hotel
and Museum collection

Occidental Room Keys
A box of room keys found in the Occidental. The presence of several different key types suggests a wide range of times during which they were used.

Source: Occidental Hotel and Museum collection

Margaret Smith's Shoes
These old shoes presumably belonged to Margaret Smith. They are on an open-wall exhibit at the Occidental Hotel Museum.

Source: Occidental Hotel and Museum collection

Occidental Restaurant Menu
An early, post-1900 restaurant menu from the Occidental dining room. A
Merchant's Lunch was 40 cents and 65 cents would buy a T-Bone Steak. The
menu is typewritten, suggesting a post-1900 date as both Remington and
Underwood typewriters were widely available during the early 20th century.

Source: Occidental Hotel and Museum collection

Occidental Tales, Fables, and Folklore

For any building, especially a public one which has been in use for over a century, it is virtually certain there will be "stories" associated with it. These stories are generally based on varying amounts of truth and they tend to evolve. They can be based on fact – tales – or on imagination – fables – or by stories preserved orally – folklore. The stories about the Occidental Hotel are no exception to this truism.

The following are several accounts for the Occidental. The author will not specify which is tale, fable, or folklore but leave that task to the reader's judgment.

A Congressman Is Serenaded at the Occidental

The October 16, 1919 *Buffalo Bulletin* carried the story of an incident at the Occidental that occurred in the early 1900s. It involved Wyoming Congressional Representative Frank Mondell and a group of cowboys at the hotel's barroom.

Frank Wheeler Mondell (1860-1939) was the Congressional Representative from Wyoming for 13 two-year terms 1895-1897 and 1899-1923. His longevity in Congress attests to his popularity in the state. The following somewhat flowery, tongue-in-cheek letter to the editor relates an incident in Mondell's frontier experiences. He had told the story years later to a friend, Prince Albert Gatchell, who wrote the letter.

WILD AND WOOLY WEST
An incident in the life of Hon. Frank Mondell.

Mr. Mondell had occasion to visit Buffalo, making the trip from the railroad station at Clearmont, Wyo., to Buffalo, a distance of some 35 miles, by stage coach, more commonly styled mud wagons in those days. It so happened that on the day of his arrival that there were a goodly number of cowboys in town that had heard of Mr. Mondell's arrival, and that he was to be quartered at the Occidental. So that evening they congregated at the Occidental bar for a joyous time and anxious to pay their respects to their Congressman in due Western style. Mr. Mondell's room, was over the barroom, and he could over hear some of their talks, such as, "Let's go up and get him. Let's have him down here."

And other kindred remarks punctuated with the usual Western emphasis. Well, as near as he could figure out their intention, they were coming up to his room. He was confronted with the fact that he was entirely unarmed – not even a pocket knife – a broken lock on the door: no bolt; so he concluded to barricade his door by using the bureau, washstand and the bed by pushing them against the door, and if worse came to worse, he would try to make his escape out the window overlooking Clear Creek, which rippled past the side of the hotel. He was finally satisfied they were coming up to his room when he heard them say, "Let's go up to his room." To make the situation more clear [sic] I will remark that the stairs led up from the office with a boxed-in stairway. These stairs led up to along hallway, on either side of which there were rooms. Mr. Mondell's room was on the left hand side, about two-thirds of the distance down the hall. He heard them as they reached the top of the stairway. There occurred a whispered consultation, one partly to give the location of the room. Silently they moved down the hall until they came in front of Mondell's room; then the party who was apparently bossing the gang, whispered: "Here we are. All ready. Let her go Gallagher."

Mondell, with nerves all tense, listened for the expected gunplay salute. Another whispered command. "Open 'er up, Shorty," meant to Mondell that the fireworks would soon commence; when in the tense silence, Shorty, in obedience to the last orders, did open up – but with what! Not with a gun fusillade, but there fell upon his ears the soothing strains of "Home, Sweet Home," rendered on a mouth harp, in musical parlance known as a harmonica. Thus was the anticipated fear turned to a musical realization – a serenading party. While the actual situation was a great relief, Mr. Mondell for a moment, was in a quandary as to what the situation demanded. He could not invite them in without exposing his barricade. But some recognition must be made. So he opened the

Frank W. Mondell – Wyoming Congressman
Frank Mondell represented Wyoming in the
late 1800s and early 1900s. He was an active
Congressman – Majority Leader of the 66th
and 67th Congress and chairman of the 1924
Republican National Convention.
Source: Modified after Website: bioguide.congress.gov.

door slightly and said, "Boys, this sure is an unexpected but agreeable surprise. I would like to invite you in but I am very tired after a long trip, and if you will excuse me I will see you boys in the morning."

"All right, Mr. Mondell, good night," came the response as they took their departure. Mr. Mondell responded most heartily, "Good night, boys."

The letter writer is the father of Buffalo's pharmacist and historian, Jim Gatchell. Prince Albert was his given name and his career was equally unusual: newspaper publisher, lawyer, Registrar of the U.S. Land Office, Justice of the Peace, Postmaster, and Adjutant General of Wyoming. His public writings were few and this is a good one.

A Rancher Departs the Occidental by Raft

An article titled "Do You Remember?" in the May 4, 1922, *Buffalo Bulletin,* reminisced about the 1895 Clear Creek Flood through Buffalo. Its principal account had to do with a Johnson County rancher escaping the floodwaters from the Occidental on an unusual raft. That portion of the newspaper article follows:

Do you remember the first flood in Clear Creek? It occurred on July 30, 1895. The crest of the flood came down about one o'clock in the afternoon. The old log Occidental hotel stood where the new Occidental now stands, but the old building was some four or five feet lower on its foundation than the new one. There was heavy wooden platform twelve feet wide and about seventy-five feet long, which served as a pavement in front to the hotel. While some of the late diners were still at the table, Dannie Mitchell came running down the alley along the south bank of the creek, just across from the hotel, calling that a great flood was coming with a wall of water ten feet high. The people in the hotel made a rush for the high ground, and in a few moments the flood came sweeping through the hotel carrying tables, chairs, and dishes and all other furniture down the creek.

E. D. Metcalf at that time kept a store in what was known as the old Lander building where C. L. Rush now does business. There was a heavy wooden platform before that building also, which served as pavement. The water ran over the lower end of this platform but did not cover it. While we were watching the swirling brown flood, the great wooden platform in front of the hotel lifted and began to float away, but near the middle of the street it seemed to get into an eddy and finally floated back and bumped against the hotel. The hotel was apparently deserted, but just as the platform touched the building, Mr. J. N. Penrose, one of the prominent ranchers of those days, climbed aboard of it from an upper window. He walked to the end of the floating ark and called out something that we understood meant he was about to take to the water and across the flood to us, but John Newell called out and warned him by motion, for the noise of the flood was very great, not to take to the water as he would surely be carried away. Mr. Newell then ran into the store and got a piece of rope and we tied a rock on one end of it, and holding the other end, threw it across the water to Mr. Penrose. He caught it and stepped from the platform into the flood. He disappeared instantly, and while we were watching the place where he went down, someone called "there he is," and we saw him struggling in water way out in the middle of the street. He had a pipe in his mouth which he continued to hold clinched in his teeth, and his hair was plastered straight back and all covered with sand and straw but he had a firm grip on the rope and we drew him to the platform in safety.

The newspapers contemporary to the flood carried other exciting stories, as would be expected, but this one was not found among them.

The Occidental's Bordello Trail

The matter of live-in prostitutes at the Occidental Hotel is a controversial one. Those individuals who hold a view of either "yes" or "no" firmly believe that they are correct.

Local historian Bob Edwards is highly skeptical that such activities took place in the Occidental, principally because of what he has learned of the character and business practices of manager Margaret Smith Bowman. Granddaughter Margaret Smith-Braniff points out that such an activity is contradictory to everything she and her siblings know about Margaret Smith from their lifelong association – she just would not have tolerated it. Margaret Smith-Braniff goes on to note that a second red light location, in addition to the well-known Laurel Avenue

Bordello Trail Stairs

The risers show concave abrasions. It is believed that the spur rowels worn by generations of cowboys departing the crib area made them. The steps were deliberately not refinished during restoration to preserve this unique effect.

Source: Author's collection

houses, was really not needed in the small Buffalo community. Also, county ranchers often brought their wives and children with them to stay at the Occidental and would not have done so had ladies of the evening been in the same building. Finally, the author has discussed this topic with a number of Buffalo old-timers whose knowledge and opinions he holds in high regard. They have lived their entire lives in Buffalo and are credible witnesses. They uniformly agree with Bob and Margaret. Thus, a family member, an independent historian, and several long-time residents have all come to the same emphatic conclusion concerning prostitution in the Occidental Hotel: "No way!"

The Wexo's have become convinced to the contrary by accounts from their visitors and guests about live-in working girls at the hotel. The principal witness was a Miss Lilly, no last name given, who visited the hotel in 2005. She was quite elderly and had a younger lady companion with her. The story Miss Lilly told was fascinating and quite detailed. She said that she was the daughter of one of the working girls who lived at the hotel during the 1920s. Her return visit after all those childhood years was obviously such an emotional experience as to give her account credibility. It seemed to Dawn Wexo that it would be virtually impossible for an elderly lady to fake such emotions – and – to what purpose?

There were reportedly two areas at the hotel, each with its own class of prostitutes where they lived and worked. One was a "bordello" that consisted of three cribs or small rooms on the second floor of the hotel's north wing, on the back side and out of sight from the hotel front. The girls there cost $3, but that included a bath, boots blackened, and longjohns washed. The hotel laundress washed the underwear and then dried them on the boiler to get them ready in a relatively short amount of time. The other working girl area was a small, separate building behind the hotel called the "annex" – nothing to do with the hotel's large, component buildings. This annex had few furnishings or amenities and the girls there cost 50 cents. Miss Lilly's mother apparently worked in that facility.

The story of resident prostitutes at the Occidental received strong, credible support from one of Buffalo's favorite centenarians, the late Verna Burger Davis. At a visit to the Occidental, Dawn Wexo said that Verna pointed out the same crib rooms that Miss Lilly had.

The name "Bordello Trail" was coined by the Wexos to describe the route that cowboys took to visit their favorite soiled dove. It begins at an outside, ground-level door at the back of the hotel. Immediately inside and to the right was the Madam's room. She was said to be a very large woman, at least 250 pounds, and could not climb stairs; therefore, her room was on the first floor. The cowboys would check in with her, and if they had the three dollars, they were sent up one flight of stairs to the crib area. If not, they were sent to the annex area out back. The Madam handled the transfer of funds and regulated traffic.

A unique feature of the Bordello Trail is on the steps to the second floor. The risers, the vertical boards that support the horizontal stair treads, are scored with multiple, concave scrapings up to a quarter-of-an-inch deep. These abrasions appear to have been made by generations of spur rowels on the cowboys' boots as they walked down the stairs to depart the crib area!

There are, of course, statements in multiple publications that could be construed, inferred, or deduced to be in support of the presence of soiled doves at the Occidental. As an example, Edith Chappell wrote in her History of the Occidental: "... about 1885, Buell and McCray acquired possession of a small hotel and converted it into a family hotel for guests of more quiet proclivities." Was she referring only to rowdy cowboys in a tavern?

Yes or no? The preceding is the author's honest attempt to present a fair and balanced account of what reliable information he has been able to uncover on this topic. Clearly, there is, at this stage, no "proof" either way.

Occidental Ghosts and Spirits

Stories of ghosts and spirits in the Occidental are part of its mystique. Completed in 1910, the century-old, brick building would be remiss in not being haunted. Probably the most notable is Emily, the seven-year-old daughter of an Occidental resident. Emily is said to have died of cholera around the turn of the 20th century. She communicates with the living by voice, saying, e.g., "Please hold me," and by touch, e.g., pushing people in the back in a playful manner. Dawn Wexo says she has seen and heard her twice. Emily was not speaking directly to her but to one of the workmen in the hotel. A medium called in some years back to contact Emily succeeded and was told that all she needed to soothe her was an "orange kitten." A stuffed, orange kitten was purchased and sits today on a radiator of the kitchen in the north wing. Hopefully, this has helped to calm Emily's spirit, but she still makes her presence known from time to time.

The spirit in the hotel's south wing was apparently a bit much more rambunctious – a bit of poltergeist. There are reports of a guest leaving at three a.m. because of furniture in his room moving about in a strange manner with no visible cause. Others heard three steps in the hallway and then a knocking on doors; always exactly three steps were heard with no one present in the hall.[32]

The Occidental in Print and on Television

Any self-respecting, historic hotel should certainly have multiple appearances over the years in the various public media, especially in print and on television. The Occidental is not deficient in this regard. Its unique status as a full-service, first-class hotel in the sparsely settled northeastern portion of Wyoming has virtually assured its popularity.

Gathering the numbers of printed articles and television program appearances about the Occidental Hotel is difficult and inherently inexact. Such was not attempted here. Rather, the library and archival research conducted to develop the hotel's history is used as a sampling of its printed exposures. That survey follows and it should provide a representative view of public media exposure.

Newspapers

The Wyoming Newspaper Project has recently converted state newspapers between 1849 and 1922 from microfilm to an Internet digital format. A search of the *Big Horn Sentinel* (1885-1889), the *Buffalo Bulletin* (1890-1923) and the *Buffalo Voice* (1897-1919) for the word "Occidental" gave a total of 3,300 hits. That includes, of course, the hotel's advertisements over the years.

Newspaper coverage has been essential in developing the history presented here. Particularly between 1889 and 1916, i.e., between the Buell and Smith family ownership periods, local newspapers provided the vast majority of the information that was available on the Occidental.

Magazine Articles

Magazine interest in the Occidental Hotel has increased markedly with the restoration process that started in 1997. Primarily, travel magazines have "discovered" the superb hotel-museum combination that exemplifies the "Old West." There is so much history and information that it is relatively easy for talented writers to produce interesting articles. Several of these were used herein; see the References listing.

Examples of the travelogue type of article have appeared in *GRIT* (2002), *Cowboys and Indians* (2003), *The Fence Post* (2005), *Wyoming Homes and Living Magazine* (2005), *Traveler Stay List* (2009), and *National Geographic Traveler Magazine* (April 2009). National and state newspapers are not to be overdone; see *The Los Angles Times* (July 2004), *The Casper Star-Tribune* (January 2005), and *The New York Times* (June 2006).

Professional Journals

The relevant journals here are those in the *Annals of Wyoming* series. It was founded in 1923 as the *Quarterly Bulletin* but changed its name two years later. Currently, the Wyoming State Historical Society in association with the Wyoming State Parks & Cultural Resources Department, the American Heritage Center, and the Department of History, University of Wyoming, publish it quarterly. The *Annals of Wyoming* had Occidental Hotel articles in 1934 (vol. 6), 1935 (vol. 7), 1939 (vol. 11), 1941 (vol. 13), and 1955 (vol. 27). Clearly, the grand "old lady" has not been neglected by Wyoming's professional historians.

The Sentry is the quarterly magazine for the Gatchell Museum Association, Inc., the foundation supporting the Jim Gatchell Memorial Museum. Each issue features articles written about local and regional history. Four Occidental articles have been published in *The Sentry* – 1997 (vol. 7), 2002 (vol. 11; two articles), and 2006 (vol. 15). Local historians are also contributing to the historic record on the Occidental Hotel.

Books

An historic hotel should certainly have books written about it in addition to the usual magazine and newspaper articles. Such is the case for the Occidental Hotel.

There is a fictional mystery entitled *Occidental Justice* written by Johnson County ranchers, Van Irvine and his daughter Sunny Irvine Taylor. It deals with the murder of a U.S. Senator in the Occidental Hotel about the turn of the 20th century that draws much attention to Buffalo and the nation's capitol. The Introduction implores the reader not to read the last page first so this writer will honor the spirit of that request. The book incorporates interesting, local details and the dialogue is presented in a sprightly manner; the story moves along nicely. Published by the authors, the book is not widely available but it is worth the effort to contact the Johnson County Library or the authors for access to a copy.

Emily and her fellow spirits that roam the halls of the Occidental on some dark nights are featured in the book, *Haunted Hotels of the West* by Bruce Raisch.

A pictorial history is presented by the *Images of America Series: Buffalo* published by the Arcadia Publishing Company. Written by the author of this work, it features a historic picture of the Occidental on its cover, as well as several other hotel photographs and discussions in the text. Introduced in 2009, it has been well received by Buffalo and Johnson County residents.

The Occidental's principal literary claim-to-fame is undoubtedly Owen Wister's 1902 classic, *The Virginian: A Horseman of the Plains*. It has been maintained for decades that the hotel provided the setting for the climactic shootout between the Virginian and Trampas.

Reportedly, the advertisements for the hotel promptly added "Where the Virginian got his Man" after the book came out. However, the earliest such published reference found by the author was a 1917 column in the *Buffalo Voice*. In an article entitled "Some Scenes of 'The Virginian'," author Robert W. Ritchie writes:

> It was the Occidental Wister selected as background for his story's swift climax. Thither the Virginian brought Molly Wood from Bear Creek schoolhouse, and it was alone in her room there the Vermont girl heard the three shots which signalized the working out of a man's code beyond even her lover to say or alter. Modern Buffalo – the townwith the prim electric lights along the cement sidewalks and the hoot of the engine whistle at its borders – displays a photographic reprint of the old log Occidental. 'Where the Virginian Got His Man' is the legend across the bottom.

The validity of the Wister-Occidental connection is now as firmly established as folklore can make it. This author has found no *documentary proof* that Wister stayed at the Occidental Hotel or that it was used as the literary site where "the Virginian got his man."

There was, however, correspondence in the early 1930s between Wister and Buffalo historian, Howard B. Lott, that bears on this matter. There is a copy of a September 18, 1931, letter from Wister to Lott that deals with the geography that Wister used for *The Virginian*. A transcription of that letter follows:

Sep. 18. 1931
Rokeby
Barrytown on Hudson

Dear Mr. Lott:

Your note has found me in the midst of some visits to friends. Yes, I had the pleasure of knowing your father in June 1891, and the ___ seeing too little of him. It's hard to answer your question. Almost all of the geography of The Virginian is imaginary, except where such names are sometimes used. I meant to indicate – but very vaguely – the Big Horn Mountains by the "Bow Leg" – and I never meant Judge Henry's ranch to be any definite ranch. I implied it as being somewhere in Johnson County – 'Bear Creek' was not intended to be any definite creek. Before writing this book, I had made a number of visits to Wyoming, and had ridden about in the Casper area, and the Wind River country, and from the Elkhorn railway up to Buffalo and was also on the west side of the Divide in Jackson's Hole and all that country. So you may say I had it all in mind generally, but ____ particularly, except where real names occur. 'Dry Bone' was short for old Fort Fetterman – no real person is in the book, unless Dr. Barber, once Governor – and I think he comes into his ____.

Your _____

Owen Wister

(Note: At the time of publication, Rokeby is an estate and Barrytown a hamlet within the Hudson River Historic District of New York.)

This was an obvious place for Wister to have mentioned the Occidental and he did not.

The correspondence between Wister and Lott was ongoing to some extent as there is an envelope to Lott dated January 25, 1932 from Philadelphia. Its contents have not been found.

There is another account of Wister's stays in the Buffalo area. According to Margaret Smith-Braniff, her grandmother Margaret Smith said that Wister was a good friend of the Eaton family and stayed at their guest ranch at Wolf Creek west of Sheridan on a regular basis. During his stays there, Wister reportedly visited the Occidental and sat out front, in the lobby, or in the bar to observe the local citizenry and absorb the "western culture." Margaret Smith indicated that he "got his man" during those observations, meaning that he got the idea of the "man" from one of the patrons at the Occidental.

The author has no problem believing the story but has been unable to find any corroboration of the Occidental's influence on Wister's fiction. Folklore certainly has its place as much of it is true, but the historical record should be as accurate and specific as possible.

Television

The Occidental Hotel has appeared several times in various television documentary and travel programs. Records of these telecasts are difficult to find. A recent Wyoming PBS program, "Wyoming Portraits," produced by Dennis Rollins, aired on February 28, 2010, featured the hotel. This half-hour program begins with a brief review of the Occidental's early history and then continues with Dawn Wexo and historian Bob Edwards commentaries of the restoration process and its success with video of the hotel's present attractive interior. The final portion of the program deals with its present-day role as a social center of Buffalo with western music events, history conferences, weddings, etc.

The Occidental's Presidential Guests

The list of famous visitors to the Occidental is impressive, if not well documented. Three suites are named for Owen Wister, Teddy Roosevelt, and Herbert Hoover. This is entirely to be expected as it was a first class, full service hotel in sparsely settled northeastern Wyoming. The more the travelers were accustomed to comfortable living the more apt they were to stay at the Occidental.

Presidential visitors are always special and there were two – Theodore Roosevelt and Herbert Hoover – who stayed at the Occidental. Their visits were separated by a half-century: Roosevelt in 1884 and Hoover in 1937.

Famous Occidental Guest – Theodore Roosevelt (1858-1919)
This undated photograph of a young Teddy Roosevelt is obviously in the West
but a specific location is not given. His young age appears about right for his
1884 Wyoming Big Horns hunt.   Source: Occidental Hotel and Museum collection

***Famous Occidental Guest –
Herbert Hoover (1899-1961)***
President Hoover was in office
1929-1933 as the 31st President
of the U.S. He visited Buffalo and
stayed at the Occidental in 1937.

Source: Occidental Hotel
and Museum collection

***President Hoover at
the Occidental***
President Hoover visits
with Johnson County
locals in the Occidental
lobby and his registration
signature at the hotel.

Source: Occidental Hotel and
Museum collection

Roosevelt was not President when he visited the hotel but had just been re-elected to a second term as a New York Assemblyman. He was 26 years old at the time and was out west in 1884 to establish two cattle ranches in the Dakota Territory. As soon as the ranches were started, Roosevelt announced that he was off on an extended exploration and hunting trip to the Big Horn Mountains – a three-day trip to the southwest. His primary quarry was what he considered the true king of the Rockies – the grizzly bear – a large member of the brown bear family. Roosevelt was successful and shot a nine-foot tall, 1,200 pound specimen with which he was delighted. He continued to collect trophies until it was necessary to rest both the hunters and their hard-working horses.

Roosevelt and his party arrived in Buffalo on September 18 and rented rooms at the Occidental. That evening they dined with the U.S.

Cavalry officers at Fort McKinney and were treated to stories concerning the northern Cheyenne. Other than the Fort McKinney visit, very little is known of Roosevelt's visit. After a recouping period in Buffalo, Roosevelt and his party returned to his ranch in the Dakota Territory.[33]

Hoover was also not President when he visited Buffalo; his term as 31st President was 1929-1933. He was a geologist by training and had worked at gold mines in this country and abroad, particularly Australia and China. He served under President Harding during World War I in various capacities. Hoover won the national presidential election in 1928. The stock market crashed the following year giving him a very difficult presidency. Defeated for re-election by Franklin D. Roosevelt in 1932, he retired to his home in California.

According to the *Buffalo Bulletin*, August 12, 1937, Hoover was en route to his home in Palo Alto, California, when he visited Buffalo and stayed at the Occidental. After touring Yellowstone Park, he visited with F. O. Horton at his HF Bar Ranch in the Big Horns. Hoover and his party then spent a day in Buffalo and left for Sheridan by automobile and on to Palo Alto.

There is a charming story of Hoover fishing with a small boy during his visit to Buffalo. It starts with the visit of an elderly man and his wife to the Occidental in 1999, some two years after the Wexos had arrived in Buffalo and began their restoration. The first floor was operated as a museum, and the doors to the rooms were left open to allow visitors to look in and go into the rooms if they wished. Dawn Wexo saw an elderly man looking about in the hallway and into the rooms. The old-timer had obviously been there before and was remembering that occasion. When Dawn moved to greet the man she saw tears were streaming down his cheeks. Dawn heard him say, "It's just as I remember it – it's just as I remember it!"

His wife responded, "You mean that crazy story you've been telling me all these years is true?"

Dawn introduced herself and asked him to tell her his Occidental story. He explained the basis for his emotion was the memory of fishing in Clear Creek with President Hoover when he was quite young. It seems that his parents were cattle ranchers in the Cheyenne area and needed to make occasional trips to Buffalo for business purposes. He and his three brothers always vied for the single place available to accompany them on those long trips and it was his turn. After checking in at the Occidental, the parents told him to take his fishing pole and go to the stream next to the hotel and they would

Hoover and Buffalo Locals in front of the Occidental
(Left to right); Dr. John Hynds, Burton S. Hill, President Hoover, and John C. Flint.

Source; *Buffalo Bulletin*, 1995, Heritage, Special Edition

President Hoover fishing – Clear Creek?
Source: Occidental Hotel and Museum collection

**Famous Occidental Guest –
Owen Wister (1860-1938)**
Source: Occidental Hotel
and Museum collection

**Owen Wister Letter to Howard
B. Lott – September 18, 1931**
This handwritten letter discusses the
geography and individuals behind
those presented in *The Virginian*. The
Occidental is not mentioned.
Source: Johnson County Library

be back later in the day when their business was finished. He did so
and was enjoying the day on streamside when an elderly gentleman
came and sat down next to him. He, of course, asked the man who
he was and was told, "They call me Mr. H." They spent the afternoon fishing as the man got his pole and joined the boy.

When the boy's parents returned, he saw how surprised and impressed they were with his fishing buddy. Finally, when they addressed the elderly man as "Mr. President" he realized that he had been fishing with a former President of the United States! Earlier that memorable day, the man had taken him in the hotel to show him his room – which is where he was now standing – some 60 years later! What a delightful memory....

That room is now numbered 55, and both it and its furniture are tied to Hoover's 1937 visit. In preparation for that occasion, two rooms on the first floor, each with a bath, had been altered to create one room with a bath and a sitting room. The elderly man recognized the furniture, especially the couch and the radio, in the room. The Wexos had gone to considerable effort to get the original furniture back into each of the rooms and enlisted the help of Buffalo old-timers, e.g., Vera Burger Davis and Jim Dillinger. The couch has a large rip in it that Dawn was going to have re-upholstered as the horsehair stuffing was starting to come out. She then found out that the rip in the couch was *caused* by President Hoover and she decided to leave it untouched. It seems that he had the habit of carrying fishing gear of all kinds in his back pocket, and this would from time to time cause tears in the furniture; supposedly even in the White House. His wife had pieces of leather sewn on the inside of his pockets to protect her mate's posterior from injury.

Occidental Windows Are Not Deer-Proof

A post-restoration assault on the Occidental was conducted by one of Buffalo's resident deer. As described by the *Buffalo Bulletin* (June 30, 2005), the animal was on Main Street at 5:30 a.m. when a loud truck approached and frightened it. The deer, in panic to escape the large, fast-moving predator, ran through the hotel's large, glass front door. Once inside, the deer's situation did not improve as it encountered a dead end. Not to be intimidated, it turned and ran out of the hotel – through the large, plate glass window to the right of the door – and on to freedom. Glass shards were scattered both inside and outside the hotel.

The deer did not, however, escape unharmed as there was some blood mixed with the glass pieces on the hotel floor. No *corpus delicti* was subsequently found so it was assumed the deer was not seriously injured.

Deer – 2, Occidental Windows – 0.

Postscript

The Occidental Hotel's future certainly looks good. More than a decade of hard work and investment has brought it back as a first rate hotel and museum. The number of hotel guests continues at a good level with an increasing percentage of out-of-state and foreign visitors. The museum also enjoys excellent visitation and it is encouraging when individuals tell how they stopped in Buffalo specifically to visit the Occidental Museum.

To those with an appreciation of the frontier history of Buffalo and Johnson County, the return of its principal icon to full operational status is good news, indeed.

Famed Western Artist
Paints the Occidental

Jesse Wilson Winingar, Jr. (1893-1960) was a Western artist renowned for his oil paintings and ink line sketches. His paintings are on exhibit throughout the country, including galleries in San Francisco and Chicago, and they are sold on both east and west coasts. Additionally, he published cowboy articles and poetry, e.g., "Bunkhouse Yarns" in <u>True West</u> *magazine in 1945.*

Winingar Painting of the Occidental
Signature Close-Up – Late 1980s
Source: Johnson County Library

J. W., as he signed his paintings, was a local boy, born on the Red Cliff ranch some 30 miles south of Buffalo. As a teenager, he began working on roundups and winter camps as a cowboy helper and then at the HF Bar as a dude wrangler. He started painting as a hobby and often chose subjects of interest to his friends and then gave them the paintings. He attended an art institute in Chicago for two years and then returned to Johnson County. He joined the Marines in World War I and in 1918 married Adeline Mary Martin. He ranched on Pole Creek, south of Buffalo, until 1941 and then went to work at the nearby Soldiers and Sailors Home of Wyoming.

Winingar began painting professionally in 1944 and continued to both give paintings to friends and sell to dealers. In 1957, he illustrated the **Buffalo Bulletin** *series, "When Wyoming Was Young," by John R. Smith, pioneer rancher, with his ink line drawings.*

Exactly when he painted the Occidental scene illustrated here is not known, but it was sometime in the late 1800s. He gave the painting to Andrew W. Kennedy who is the nearest man on a horse. It is now owned by Kennedy's great-grandson, Michael, of Texas. It was apparently the inspiration for the Occidental Hotel Christmas card used years later and shown below.

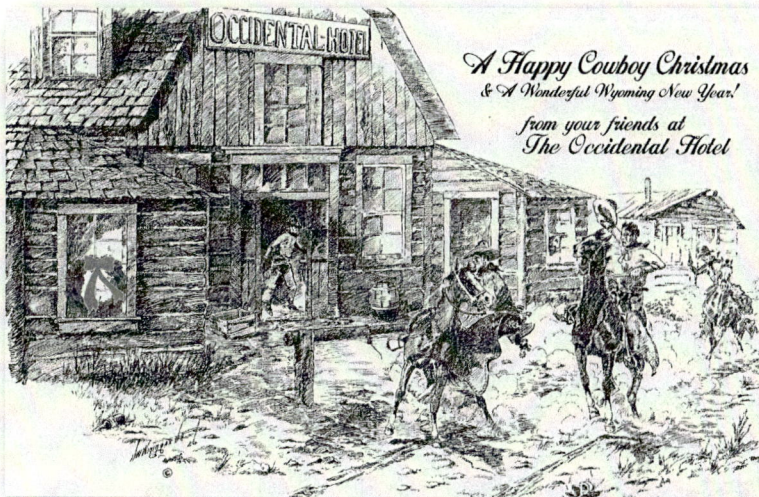

Occidental Christmas Card – 1990s.
Source: Johnson County Library

The Last Big Horn Grizzly

The story of Teddy Roosevelt bagging a large grizzly in the Big Horn Mountains is exciting, especially to hunters, as it has probably been a century since the last one was killed there. Two candidates for that last ursus artos horribilis *are presented below in the photograph and in the newspaper article.*

Source: Occidental Hotel
and Museum collection

James Morgareidge has succeeded at last in killing the old pioneer bear of Powder river. This old bear has been ranging in that section of the country for the last ten years and has killed a large number of cattle. The morning after the snow, last Saturday, Jim struck his trail on Red Fork and followed it to where he had killed a two-year-old heifer belonging to Tom Gardner. From the carcass he followed the trail a short distance and found the old fellow in Cottonwood canyon. He shot at him but missed and bruin started for him. He shot five times more and hit him four times, killing him when he was within a few feet of him. The bear made a track 18 inches long, his hide measured 9 feet 8 inches long and 8 feet 8 inches wide and he weighed 1,400 pounds. Fifteen gallons of lard were rendered from his carcass.

This photograph is labeled as a grizzly bear in the Big Horns but neither the hunters nor the year are identified. Source: Jim Gatchell Memorial Museum

This article appeared in *The People's Voice* on September 28, 1895.

Source: Author's collection.

Appendix:

Guest Registers – 1885 to 1909

Guest Registration Clippings – 1885 to 1888

Occidental Hotel guest registers for the years 1885 to 1901 were examined at the American Heritage Center, University of Wyoming, in Laramie. A total of seven registers for the following time periods: March-December 1885 (Box 1), October 1887-July 1888 (Box 2), January-October 1890 (Box 3), November 1890-August 1891 (Box 4), March 1899-January 1900 (Box 5), January 1900-January 1901 (Box 6), and January-December 1901 (Box 7). The collection's accession number is 9019.

While the preceding represents a superb resource, it is useful to realize how much is missing. For the 17 years (1885-1901), we have only 2,200 days or six years of registers. Additionally, they are all altered, i.e., they were reused by the Buffalo Pharmacy to hold prescriptions (1901-1906) that were pasted over the right-hand (odd-numbered) pages. Such re-use practices were common during that time. The result is that there are only the left hand pages (even-numbered) with useable entries – a total of three years of record for the calendar 17 years.

Following are a number of illustrations that depict portions of the pages of those guest registers. They feature names of pioneer Buffalo businessmen and Johnson County ranchers who were important in the frontier history of the area. At least one registrant is identified on each page. See how many others you can recognize.

Guest Registration Clippings – 1899 to 1909

In addition to the previously mentioned registers in the American Heritage Center, the Occidental Hotel collections include four registers for the time periods: January 1 to September

18, 1903; September 19, 1903 to July 6, 1904; July 4, 1904 to April 3, 1905; and August 27, 1908 to April 8, 1909. Cropped views from those registers are shown in the following.

The Wyoming State Archives hold one Occidental guest register. It is for the year 1887 which is missing at the American Heritage Center. It is available on microfilm under their Historical Collections category, and the author obtained a copy.

These three sets, 12 registers from the Occidental Hotel, Wyoming State Archives, and American Heritage Center collections, are all of the early era guest registers that have been found by the author.

In viewing the register signatures, it is important to note that, in some instances, the hotel clerk would sign a known guest into the register; it is sometimes difficult to know if this has happened or if it is, indeed, the guest's signature. Comparison with adjacent entries is often helpful in this regard.

Again, on the following pages, at least one registrant signature is identified.

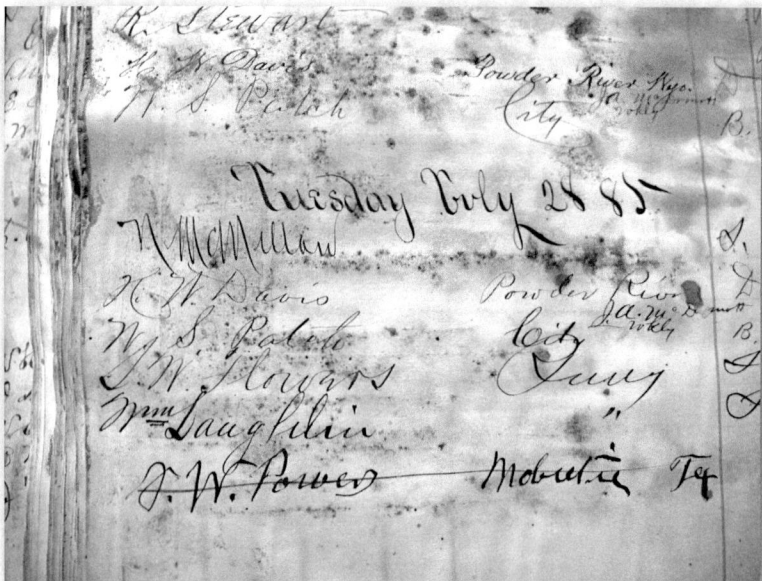

H. W. Davis – July 28, 1885
"Hard" Winter Davis – Cattle Baron and erstwhile Cattle War Invader.
The name appears twice; second from the top of the illustration and second in the Tuesday listing.

Source: Occidental Hotel and Museum collection

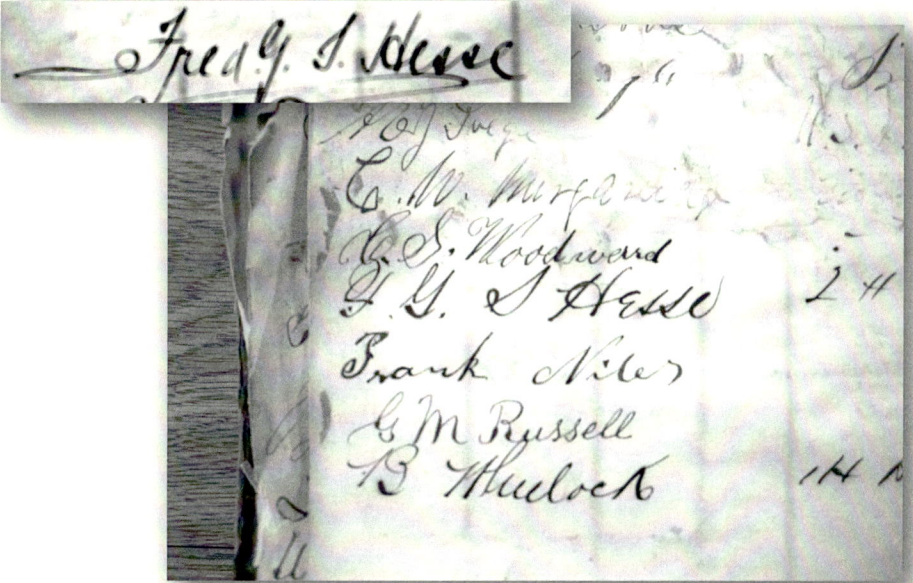

F. G. S. Hesse – circa 1888 (top) and **1885** Cattle Baron – Entrepreneur
– Cattle War Invader. This is an example of different signatures for the same
man; one or both a clerk entry?

Source: Occidental Hotel and Museum collection

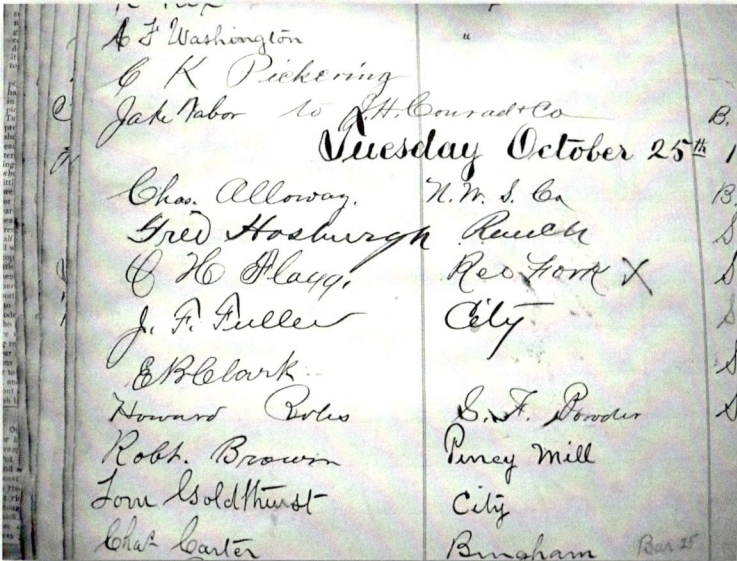

O. H. Flagg – October 25, 1887
Rancher – Newspaperman – Reputed rustler and Cattle War participant.

Source: Occidental Hotel and Museum collection

November 19, 1887
Geo. T. Beck (4th) – Entrepreneur – Partner with Bill Cody – Built first flour mill, electric generator plant and light system in Buffalo. L. A. Webb (10th) – Small rancher – A suspected leader of the rustler element in the Cattle War.

Source: Occidental Hotel and Museum collection

C. E. Buell – May 28, 1888
This date is more than a month after Buell had sold the Occidental Hotel to McCray.

Source: Occidental Hotel and Museum collection

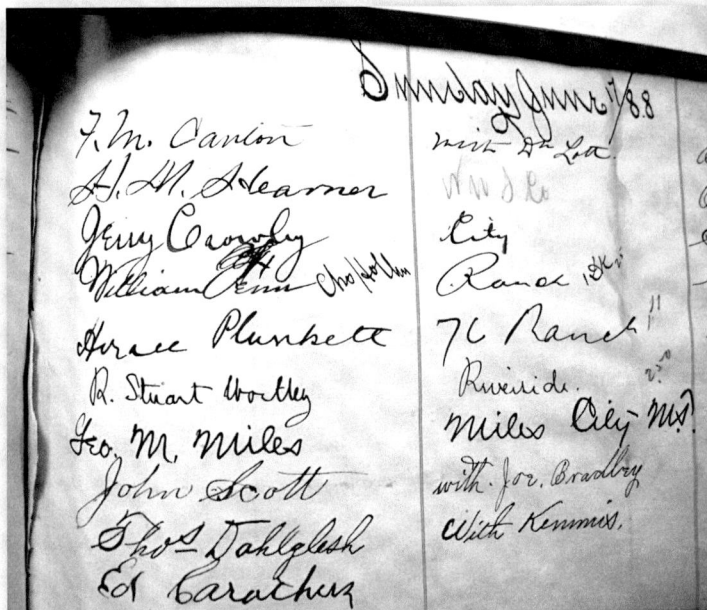

June 17, 1888
F. M. Canton (1st) – Sheriff – Stock detective, reputed killer – Cattle War Invader.
Thos. Dahlglesh (10th) – Early commercial photographer in Buffalo.

Source: Occidental Hotel and Museum collection

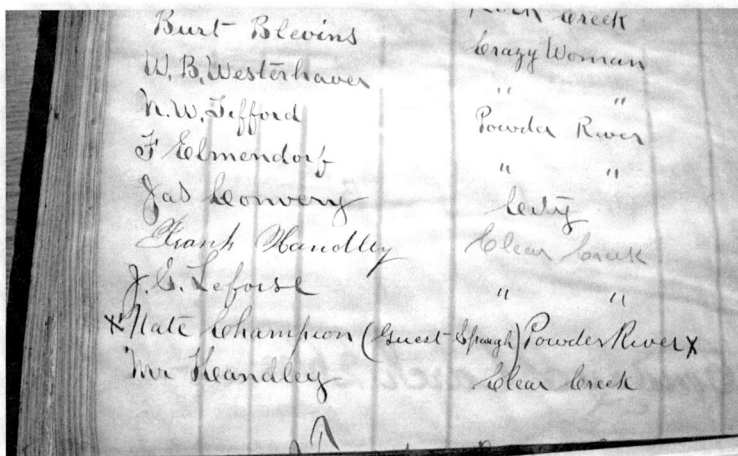

March 26, 1888
Nate Champion – Small rancher – Killed at KC Ranch – Known as "the bravest man in Johnson County." **J. E. Leforse** – Deputy U.S. Marshal – Hole-in-the-Wall gunfight participant – The man who got the confession from Tom Horn. Leforse should be spelled Lefors – Mistaken clerk entry?

Source: Occidental Hotel and Museum collection

John R. Smith – June 20, 1888
Pioneer rancher, county commissioner, and author

Source: Occidental Hotel and Museum collection

Mrs. C. E. Buell and eldest daughter, Helen – August 2, 1899
Source: Occidental Hotel and Museum collection

July 8-9, 1900

W. J. Thom – Early rancher and banker in Buffalo. **B. F. Champion** (Nate's brother) – Small rancher – Lifelong Johnson County resident.

Source: Occidental Hotel and Museum collection

O. H. Flagg – October 1, 1900

This is obviously a humorous entry as Fort McKinney was decommissioned in 1894 and Flagg was not in the Army.

Source: Occidental Hotel and Museum collection

June 5, 1903

L. A. Webb – Small rancher, a leader of the rustler element in The Cattle War.
A. S. Mercer – Newspaperman, editor, author of "Banditti of the Plains."
June 17, 1888. Upper: **Bull Creek Mike from Crazy [Woman?] Creek** –
The author has no idea who Bull Creek Mike is supposed to be.

Source: Occidental Hotel and Museum collection

A. M. Brock, Mayoworth – Pioneer rancher and historian.
Prof. Von Vreeland – Traveling entertainer. c. 1901.

Source: Occidental Hotel and Museum collection

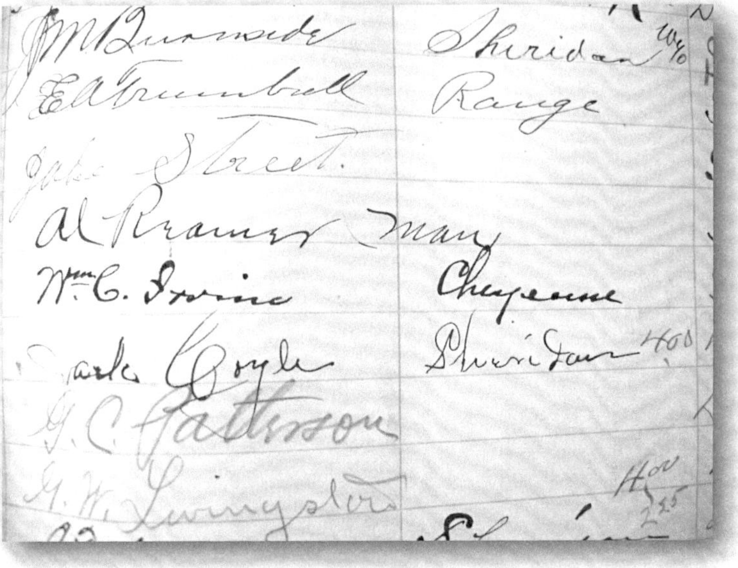

August 27, 1904
Wm. C. Irvine – Cattle baron, leader of the 1892 Invasion – politician.

Source: Occidental Hotel and Museum collection

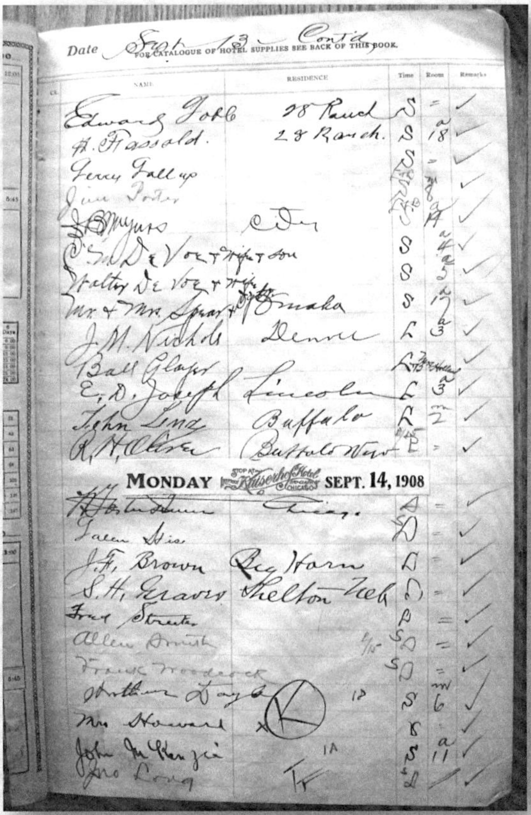

Full Register page for
September 13-14, 1908
Source: Occidental Hotel
and Museum collection

A. L. Brock, Sept. 9, 1900 and
J. Elmer Brock, Oct. 9, 1908 (top two names)

Fred G. Hesse, wife and 2, Nov. 13, 1908 (middle)

Mart Tisdale – Rancher an Johnson County Sheriff. Oct. 9, 1909.
Chas. Bolinger – Pioneer Johnson County Rancher. Jan. 31, 1908
(bottom two names).

Source: Occidental Hotel and Museum collection

References

Books

Bartlett, I. S., Ed. **History of Wyoming.** Vol. I. Chicago, IL: S. J. Clarke Publishing Company, 1918. 564-565.

Bollinger, Gil. **Jim Gatchell – The Man and the Museum.** Buffalo, WY: Gatchell Memorial Museum Press, 1999.

Bollinger, Gil and Jim Gatchell Memorial Museum. **Images of America: Buffalo.** Charleston, SC: Arcadia Publishing Co., 2009.

Bowker, Lee and Leroy L. Lenger. **Wyoming Trade Tokens.** Self-published, 1999.

Brinkley, Douglas. **The Wilderness Warrior.** New York, NY: HarperCollins, 2009.

Buffalo's Centennial Book Committee. **Buffalo's First Century.** Buffalo, WY: Buffalo's Centennial Book Committee, 1984.

Buell, Helen. "The Occidental Hotel." **Buffalo's First Century.** Buffalo's Centennial Book Committee. Buffalo, WY: Buffalo's Centennial Book Committee, 1984. 15-16.

DeArment, Robert K. **Alias Frank Canton.** Norman, OK: University of Oklahoma Press, 1996. 242-243.

Edwards, Robert C. **Guns of the Gatchell.** Buffalo, WY: Jim Gatchell Memorial Museum Press, 2009. 89-111.

Gallagher, John S., and Alan H. Patera. **Wyoming Post Offices.** WY: The Depot, 1980.

Hanson, Margaret B. **Powder River Country: the Papers of J. Elmer Brock.** Kaycee, WY: Self-published, 1981. 166-167, 467-469.

Heald, George D. **Wyoming Flames of ~'92.** WY: Self-published, 1972.

Irvine, Van and Sunny Irvine Taylor. **Occidental Justice.** Self-published.

Murray, Robert A. **Johnson County – 175 Years of History at the Foot of the Big Horn Mountains.** 1981. Buffalo, WY: Jim Gatchell Memorial Museum Press, 2003. 61.

O'Neal, Bill. **The Johnson County War.** Austin, TX: Eakin Press, 2004.

Raisch, Bruce A. **Haunted Hotels of the West.** Virginia Beach, VA: The Donning Co., 2009. 87-88.

Newspapers

Big Horn Sentinel: 1885 to 1889

Buffalo Bulletin: 1890 to 2009

Buffalo Voice: 1897 to 1919

Casper Star Tribune: 2005

New York Times: 2006

People's Voice: 1892 to 1897
 (Above runs not all complete)

Magazines and Journals

Aughenbaugh, Anna. "The Occidental Hotel." *Fence Post* (October 18, 2005): 4-7.

Bedor, Mark. "Wyoming Hotel Takes a Step Back in Time." *GRIT Magazine* (December 22, 2002): 20-21.

_____. "Occidental Hotel." *Cowboys and Indians* (March 2003): x.

Bollinger, Gil. "A Condemned Poet." *The Sentry* Vol. 11, No. 3 (July 2002) 4-6.

_____. "The Fort, the Town, and the Lady." *The Sentry* Vol. 15, No. 2 (April 2006) 1-4.

Bollinger, Gil and Joan Smith. "Special Lady – Special Hotel." *The Sentry* Vol. 7, No. 3 (July 1997): 1-3.

Chappell, Edith M. "History of the Occidental Hotel." *Annals of Wyoming* Vol. 1, No. 2 (April 1939) 128-132.

Condit, Thelma Gatchell. "The Hole-in-the-Wall." *Annals of Wyoming* (1966): 175-192.

Edwards, Bob. "W. G. 'Red' Angus." *The Sentry* Vol. 11, No. 4 (July 2002): 1-3.

Karvonen, Kareen. "Buffalo Showplace: the Occidental Hotel." *Old West* (Summer 1970): 38-43.

Local History Department at the Johnson County Library. **Johnson County Library Local History Files.** These files, by subject, have been accumulated and maintained by the Library staff for decades. They are a treasure trove of Wyoming and Johnson County history.

Lott, H. B. "The Old Occidental." *Annals of Wyoming* Vol. 27, No. 1 (1955): 25-30.

Pearce, Bennett R. "Old Times at the Occidental." *Old West* (Summer 1970): 38-40, 72-73.

Zeller, Penny A. "Bringing the Past Alive." *Wyoming Homes and Living Magazine* Vol. 3, Issue 1 (Spring 2005): 56-75.

Electronic Documents

Dobson, G. B. "Buffalo Photos." Online. www.wyomingtalesandtrails.com/buffalo.html.

End Notes

The Buell Years – 1879 – 1888

1. Hanson, Margaret B., (1981), p. 166.

2. Buell, Helen (1984).

3. *Ibid*. The current and several following paragraphs follow Helen Buell's development of the Occidental history. While the cited version was published in 1984, it was actually written much earlier, probably in the late 1920s. Helen, the Buell's eldest child, was born in 1883 appropriately, in the Occidental Hotel. Thus, it is the earliest history of the hotel and, additionally, was written by a family member that grew up in it. Subsequent histories published were by Lott (1934) and by Chappell (1939). Those accounts were well done and added some new material but they were clearly based on Helen Buell's earlier account. There is a WPA paper by Mrs. Charles S. Baker, dated 1915, on file at the Johnson County Library; it mentions the skull found by Buell in site clearing.

4. *Buffalo Bulletin*, August 9, 1951, article by Lillian Baker and Bollinger, Gil, (2009), p. 15; Mickelson, Nancy, (2010), written communication (unpublished documents on the history of the Trabing Brothers).

5. William Hart (Harter?) was the first Buffalo Postmaster. *Buffalo Bulletin*, August 9, 1951, and Gallagher and Patera, (1980).

6. With respect to the first county commissioners, the name, Ray Park, is from a *Buffalo Bulletin*, March 1, 1973, article by Sue Myers; many accounts only list the other two names. Bartlett, I. S. (1918), Vol. I, see p. 564.

7. Website: Parents and Siblings of Sophie Nielsen.

8. Hanson, Margaret B., (1981), p. 166-167.

9. Bollinger, Gil, (2002), pp. 4-6.

10. Bollinger, Gil, (2006), pp. 1-4

11. Johnson County Land Abstracts and Lott, H. B. (1934), *ibid*.

12. Lott, H. B. (1934), *ibid*; Chappell, Edith M. (1939), *ibid*: and an undated *Laramie Daily Boomerang* article from the Johnson County's Red Scrapbook file.

13. Advertisements in the *Big Horn Sentinel* during November and December, 1885.

14. Jennie B. Buell's patent for 160 acres in S22-T52N-R83W was awarded on June 30, 1891 and Charles' claim, also for 160 acres, in S8-T52N-R83W came though on July 13, 1891. President Benjamin Harrison's name appeared on both patents. In 1908, Buell purchased 40 acres from the U.S. Land Office and that deed was signed by President Theodore Roosevelt. These documents are still held by Buell family descendants. The Buell accident resulting in their deaths was widely covered by regional newspapers; see the *Buffalo Bulletin*, January 27, 1916.

15. Some Occidental writers ascribe economic reasons to the frequent transfers in the ownership. For example, Chappell, (1939) cites the 1912 flood as the reason Quick and Waegele decided to sell the hotel. Perhaps, but they were five years in doing so as the sale to the Smith brothers was in 1917.

16. Listing entries are derived from the newspapers cited and from Buell (1984), Lott (1934), and Chappell (1939).

17. *The Buffalo News* of January 26, 1926, has a front page obituary for Henry A. Smith, Commandant of the Soldiers and Sailors Home, who had died a week earlier. He and his brother were born in Oregon and came to Buffalo in 1890 and took over operation of the Occidental. Henry enlisted in the Army during the Spanish American War; he returned to Buffalo and became the veteran's home Commandant.

18. Edwards, (2002), pp. 1-3; Bollinger (1999), pp. 144-145; Wyoming Tales and Trails: Johnson County War, p. 5.

19. Bollinger (1999), *ibid*; Wyoming Tales and Trails, ibid; Johnson County Library Local History files: written communication (1966), Sharon L. Field, April 5th. Brown's middle name was his mother's maiden name.

20. Edwards, (2002), *ibid*; Johnson County District Court Docket No. 1, Term Nov. 1893, State of Wyoming vs., William G. Angus, Action for Assault with attempt to commit murder.

21. Wyoming Tales and Trails, *ibid*. That source states that Brown's killers were never charged. The *Buffalo Bulletin*, March 21, 1901, states that the killers were caught by the sheriff and that they confessed. The *Buffalo Voice* of March 3, 1901, reported that both murderers pleaded guilty to second degree murder and were given life sentences. Condit (1966) p. 192, states that they were pardoned on the condition that they leave the state.

22. Condit, Thelma Gatchell (1966).

23. *Buffalo Bulletin*, Sept. 3 and 10, 1896; Pearce, (1970), p. 73.

24. Hanson, Margaret B. (1981) pp. 467-469 and DeArment, Robert K. (1996), pp. 242-243.

25. *Buffalo Bulletin*, Aug. 8, 1901.

26. Chappell, Edith M. (1939) lists the years that the three brick sections were constructed in a slightly different sequence: the 1903 construction she has begun in 1906 and called the annex, the central portion she has as built in 1908 which agrees with what is listed herein, and the south part in 1909 which is given as 1910 in the preceding.

27. Pearce, (1970), p. 73.

28. Pearce, (1970), *ibid*; Bollinger, (2009), pp. 79-80.

29. Local newspaper (*People's Voice?*), January 24, 1916; *Buffalo Bulletin*, March 10, 1916.

30. Bollinger and Smith, (1997), pp. 1-3. The Smith co-author here is a granddaughter of Margaret Smith Bowman, the long-term manager of the Occidental. Accordingly, much reliance is placed on this 1997 article. Murray, (2003 edition), see p. 61

31. The restoration information and details here were taken from the series of magazine articles in the *American Profile* (2001), *GRIT* (2002), *Fence Post* (2004), *Wyoming Homes & Living* (2005), and in the *Casper Star-Times* for January 3, 2005.

32. Carlson, Chuck. "Ghost of a Chance." **Buffalo Bulletin** (October 29, 2009): B3-B4.

33. Brinkley, Douglas, 2009, p. 171-175.

Index

G

gallows – 16
Gardner, Tom – 106
Gatchell Condit, Thelma – 39
Gatchell, Jim – ii, 36, 87, 93, 106
Gatchell Museum Association, Inc. – 93
Gatchell, P. A. – 43
Gilkey, O. A. – 30
Gossett, Dr. – 36, 37
Greub – 56
GRIT – 93
grizzly bear – 98, 106
Grouard, Frank – 29
guest ranch – 96

H

Hainer, Al – 29
Hard Winter – 108
Hart, Juliet – 6, 18
Hart, Major Verling K. – 6, 17
Hart, William – 4
Herrick, Jennie B. – 5
Hesse, Fred G. S. – 8, 109
HF Bar Ranch – 99
Hill, T. P. – 43
Hoover, Herbert – 96, 97
Horton, F. O. – 99
human skull – 2

I

Invaders – 34, 35
Irvine, Sunny – 93
Irvine, Van – 93
Irvine, Wm. C. – 115

J

Jefferson, Thomas – 5
Johnson County War – 30
Jolly, Mr. – 64
Jones, J. A. – 39

K

Kaycee – 1
Keays, W. P. – 43
Keeler, Vinnie M. – 5
Kennedy, Sheriff – 38, 39

Klinkhammer, Vincent – 62
Knowledge Company – 73

L

land abstract – 18
Lane – 7
Laurel Avenue – 35, 89
Lazy Fly – 66
Leforse, J. E. – 111
Los Angles Times, The – 93
Lott, Dr. – 8
Lott, Howard B. – 94, 101

M

Main Street Bridge – 23
Martin, Adeline Mary – 105
masquerade ball – 6
McBride, Senator Wilson – 43
McCain, Jeanette Burris – 64
McCray, Alvin J. – 4, 5
McDonald, Sam – 27
McGinnis, Peter – 38
Meeteetse – 56
Menth, H. W. – 5
Mercer, Asa S. – 30, 114
Metcalf, E. D. – 88
military surgeon – 7
Miller, Wm. – 36, 37
Miss Lilly – 90
Mitchell, Dannie – 88
Moeller, Captain G. E. A. – 43
Mondell, Frank Wheeler – 85
Morgareidge, James – 106
Morse Code – 34
Munkres, George – 43
Murray Hill Hotel – 7, 21
Murray, Robert A. – 2
Myers, G. F. – 43
Myers, Pap – 22

N

National Geographic Traveler Magazine – 93
National Register of Historic Places – 74
Newell, John – 88
New York Store – 58
New York Times, The – 93

W

Waegele, Fred – 30, 44, 53
warranty deed – 54
Webb, L. A. – 110, 114
Western Union telegraph key – 33
Wexo, Dawn – iii, 65, 73
Wexo, John – iii, 65, 73, 74
whiskey flask – 82
Wilhams, Ed – 8
Williams, Lum – 8
Willow Grove – 38, 56, 69
Winingar, Jesse Wilson Jr. – 104
Wister, Owen – 94, 95, 96, 101
Wolf Creek – 96
Wood, Molly – 94
World War I – 25, 99, 105

Wyoming Homes and Living Magazine – 93
Wyoming Newspaper Project – 92
Wyoming Portraits – 96
Wyoming State Historical Society – 78, 93
Wyoming State Parks & Cultural Resources Department – 93
Wyoming Stock Growers Association – 30, 41

Y

Yellowstone Park – 99

Z

Zindel, W. H. – 43
Zoobooks – 73